Dublin Diocesan Library
Clonliffe Road,
Dublin 3.

This book is due for return on or before the last date shown below.

-4 OCT 1988 17 SEP 2009

D1349045

MATER DEI LIBRARY

M/ 941.83 BRAD

Viking Dublin exposed : the Wood Quay sa

0 1175 737X

VIKING DUBLIN EXPOSED

The Wood Quay Saga

VIKING DUBLIN EXPOSED

The Wood Quay Saga

Edited by

JOHN BRADLEY

THE O'BRIEN PRESS

DUBLIN

First published 1984 by
The O'Brien Press Ltd., 20 Victoria Road, Rathgar, Dublin 6

©Copyright The Friends of Medieval Dublin,
B. Ó Ríordáin and P. F. Wallace. Book design and setting The O'Brien Press Ltd.
Photographs and illustrations copyright to their owners.

British Library Cataloguing in Publication Data
Viking Dublin exposed: the Wood Quay saga.
1. Northmen — Ireland — Dublin (Dublin)
2. Wrecking   3. Dublin (Dublin) — Antiquities
I. Bradley, John
941.8'35'004395   DA995.D75
ISBN 0-86278-066-7

All rights reserved. No part of
this book may be reproduced or utilised
in any form or by any means, electronic or mechanical,
including photocopying, recording or by any
information storage and retrieval system
without permission in writing
from the publisher.

Acknowledgements:
The Friends of Medieval Dublin wish to express their thanks to all
who supported the campaign to save Wood Quay but especially we
wish to thank two families for their constant help and commitment:
Nick and Mary Robinson, whose legal expertise and friendship was a
continual source of comfort and strength and the Caseys of
Fishamble Street, whose home was always open to us.
We wish to thank the *Capuchin Annual* for permission to re-publish
Breandán Ó Ríordáin's article, and *The Belvederian* in which a
portion of Fr F. X. Martin's text originally appeared.

Book design: Michael O'Brien
Cover design: Frank Spiers
Typesetting: Photo-Set Ltd.
Printing: Leinster Leader, Naas

941.83
BRAD

Contents

TO ALL
WHO FOUGHT
TO
SAVE WOOD QUAY

Foreword

The historian's business is with the past: to find out what really happened, how, when, and if possible why. For this purpose we need the remains of the past: documents (which in this century we have shown ourselves only too ready to destroy); artifacts of all kinds, which need to be recorded in their original setting; structures of all kinds, few of which have survived. To the historian the opportunity of walking the streets of a vanished city, laid out by our ancestors some thirty generations ago, before the Normans, before Brian Boru, and observing the defences they constructed, something of a kind which hardly exists elsewhere in Europe, is as precious and revealing as any document, and especially so for a period for which there is almost no documentation. To destroy it unrecorded would be a monstrous offence against historical truth; to destroy it at all, when this could be avoided, should be unthinkable. What is at stake is the evidence of the oldest urban life in Ireland: once it is gone, it is gone forever.

Jocelyn Otway-Ruthven

JOHN BRADLEY

Introduction

For over three and a half years, from August 1977 until March 1981, Wood Quay figured constantly in the headlines. A week did not pass without the site being mentioned in the national press, or on radio or television. More and more people became aware of its enormous archaeological potential and the appeals to preserve the site increased proportionately. In an unprecedented legal action the High Court declared the part of Wood Quay within the old city wall a National Monument and, in an equally unprecedented act, Dublin Corporation, the owners of the site, exploited a loophole in the law and obtained permission to demolish the National Monument. The public outcry and the campaign for preservation became all the greater, but at the end of the day Dublin Corporation had their way. The only tangible result was that those archaeological deposits which were not destroyed by the Corporation's bulldozers were carefully and systematically excavated by a team under the direction of Mr Patrick Wallace. The records made in the course of these excavations and the hundreds of thousands of artifacts which are now housed in the National Museum of Ireland will be a fundamental basis for research into Viking and medieval Dublin for many years to come.

The Wood Quay story does not end there however, nor indeed with the construction of the concrete tower blocks which now stand on the site. In fact the story is not over yet. Two court cases are still pending and the future of many of those prominent in the battle to save Wood Quay still lies in the balance. Nine individuals are being sued by John Paul & Co., a building contractor, for damages amounting to £53,610.11 arising out of the delay caused by the occupation of the site in June 1979, while Dublin Corporation is pursuing Professor F. X. Martin for £89,500 awarded to them by the Supreme Court in a separate case arising out of the delay to the building project caused by the legal action taken by him between January and March 1979. In addition, Professor Martin has lodged a case, still pending, with the European Commission on Human Rights, the circumstances of which he himself outlines in this book.

Although these court cases have not yet been concluded, the time is opportune to recount the Wood Quay story. Opportune, because the problems which made Wood Quay a public issue have not been solved. Fundamental to these problems is the fact that the Viking-medieval core of Dublin is not being recognised for what it is, an archaeological monument in its own right, an area which must be treated sensitively and where modern development must be rigidly controlled. This core was inherited. It had been the kernel of Dublin's life for centuries and consequently it was characterised by a closely-knit community and its buildings were low-rise, used, for the most part, as dwellings or small family businesses. In terms of building land however, this area is among the most valuable in the city precisely because it is so centrally placed. In some areas there were slums and understandably these were cleared; in other instances, perfectly good houses were acquired by compulsory purchase order and demolished. They were replaced, not by low-rise dwellings, but by blocks of flats, high-rise offices, and car parks. Roads, instead of being diverted around the historic core, are being widened and pushed through the old city, destroying the medieval street system and turning what remains into a series of isolated traffic islands. In the process most of the inhabitants were transplanted to the outskirts of the city, and the historic core, which should have been a life-centre, became the wasteland it is today. If cities are meant to be places in which people *live,* then Dublin's planners have failed utterly. The present derelict centre may well be a property developer's dream, but precisely because it *is* the old core, it is an archaeologist's nightmare.

Sealed underneath the modern surface are a series of archaeological layers which chronicle the story of the city from its very beginnings. These have developed because refuse was scattered during the Middle Ages – there was no rubbish collection as there is today – and because one house was built upon the foundations of another, century after century. The depth of these layers varies from place to place within the old core. In some areas it is as much as 26 feet, in others it might be only a quarter of this. The depth depends partly on proximity to the Liffey and partly on the amount of disturbance caused by the digging of cellars in Georgian and Victorian times. The range of material found in these layers and the extent of the preservation is recounted by Breandán Ó Ríordáin from the results of his own excavations throughout the city.

Wood Quay itself occupies 4½ acres within the medieval city and was chosen in 1956 as the site for the proposed Civic Offices Centre for Dublin Corporation. The land was gradually acquired and by 1968, as Richard Haworth points out, the whole site had been purchased. Although excavations commenced in 1969, the real importance of the site did not become apparent until the campaign of excavations – commenced in 1974 by Pat Wallace and whose results he summarises here – was instigated. These showed that parts of the living areas, defences, and port, of the early city were preserved on the site, ranging in date from the tenth until the early fourteenth century. Structural foundations and individual objects were in an excellent state of preservation because the archaeological layers were waterlogged. When these layers were threatened with destruction by bulldozing in 1977 the Friends of Medieval Dublin launched a campaign to ensure that the archaeological deposits would be excavated scientifically. When the excavations were resumed however, it quickly became apparent to many members of the Friends that this was no ordinary site. As feature after feature was uncovered the wealth of preserved material became clear. Accordingly the Friends of Medieval Dublin, realising that the site was of European rather than local importance, decided to try and preserve it as an archaeological monument by persuading the City Authorities to build their offices elsewhere. It was at this stage that Wood Quay became a matter of increasing public concern.

The story of Wood Quay begins in Viking times and stretches right through to

General view of Wood Quay showing excavations in progress, foreground, with the town wall on the right and building works in the background, October, 1978.

the present day. The purpose of this book is to chart that story, to outline what occurred and when, and to show how the issue developed and why the Friends of Medieval Dublin took the actions that they did. In so far as the basic subject matter of the story is Viking, the term 'saga' is a suitable one as the story has many of the qualities of a saga. The essential elements of any epic are surely that it is long, that there is a struggle between opposed forces and that it is filled with dramatic incident. The Wood Quay story certainly lacks none of these.

The legal battles and the public demonstrations come fairly late in the course of the saga however, and in Richard Haworth's chapter we discover how it came about that Wood Quay had to be fought over at all. He traces the course of events from the fateful decision in 1901 to build new civic offices, through the acquisition of the site by compulsory purchase order, to its clearing in the early 1970s prior to building. If our saga has a hero it is undoubtedly Rev F. X. Martin, o.s.a., Professor of Medieval History at University College Dublin and one of Ireland's foremost historians, whose name is synonymous to most people with that of Wood Quay. His account takes the story from 1977 to 1981, charting the gradual rise of public interest and the attempts made to preserve the site. The most dramatic incident of our story is undoubtedly the occupation of the site by twenty of Ireland's most prominent citizens in June 1979, and Bride Rosney provides a day-by-day account of that event.

The beginnings of the saga are much older than this century, of course, and Patrick Wallace takes us back to the initial Wood Quay, the very beginnings of the modern city. In the light of his post-excavation research he assesses the archaeological significance of the site and describes the range of new information which his excavations have given to knowledge of early Dublin. It

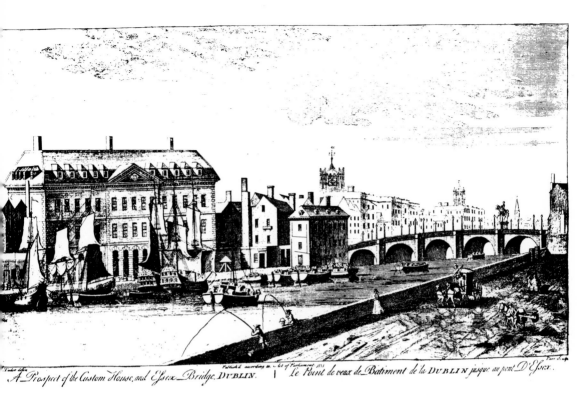

A Prospect of the Custom House, and Essex Bridge, DUBLIN. | Le Point de veux de Batiment de la DUBLIN jusque au pont D'Essex.

Left: St Patrick's Cathedral, around 1840.
Above: View of Essex Bridge with Wood Quay behind, 1753; the Old Custom House is on the left.

was Ireland's first true town and the information on its character and layout is therefore particularly important. He also highlights the significance of the site in European terms, providing a glimpse of the importance which the full excavation report, now in preparation, will have for the study of town life in medieval Europe.

Dr Howard Clarke outlines the problems which confront both the archaeologist and historian who tries to reconstruct early life in Dublin and provides us with a summary of the historical evidence, supplementing his already published papers on the subject. Anngret Simms emphasises the concept of place and the essential role which indentification with place plays in our lives. She looks also at the wider European world of which Viking Dublin formed an essential part. John de Courcy traces the course of the river Liffey on an autumn day in the year A.D. 850; it was this waterway, offering the possibilities of penetrating into the heart of Leinster that attracted the first Vikings. Indeed, just as the Volga is *Mat Reka,* mother of rivers, so too one might say that the Liffey is Dublin's progenitor.

The buildings that occupied Wood Quay prior to their purchase by Dublin Corporation form the subject of Peter Walsh's essay which he illustrates with old and rare photographs that preserve the vanished shadows of yesterday. Our concluding section looks to the future by outlining the policy which the Friends of Medieval Dublin believe should be adopted if Dublin's Viking and medieval heritage is to be adequately safeguarded and displayed. It concludes with a series of recommendations which, if adopted, will ensure that a Wood Quay *débâcle* will never happen again.

A protest march arrives at Wood Quay, 1978.

VIKING DUBLIN PLUNDERED

CHAPTER 1

RICHARD HAWORTH

The Modern Annals of Wood Quay

The modern history of the Wood Quay affair can be put back to the opening year of this century when Dublin Corporation received a proposal from its Public Libraries Committee to build a central public library at Lord Edward Street, to provide accommodation for the recently acquired Gilbert Library and 'for a museum to contain objects of local interest to the city'. The accompanying report of the city architect put the cost of this development at £28,000. When the report was considered at the following monthly meeting, an amendment, by the Lord Mayor of the day, changed the picture by proposing that 'this report be referred to the Improvements Committee to prepare a scheme at the earliest possible date for the erection of new Municipal Buildings and the rearrangement of the City Hall, and at the same time to consider if the new library could not be joined with the proposed new Municipal Buildings'; and this was approved. The change of plan found no favour with the Improvements Committee, however, and consideration of the report was postponed. Eighty years later neither the new Civic Offices nor the new Central Library have been completed.[1]

ABERCROMBIE PLAN, 1914-1950s

A competition was held in 1914 for a new town plan for 'Greater Dublin' and the winning entry, by Patrick Abercrombie and Associates, was lavishly published by the Civics Institute of Ireland in 1922. In this original plan, completed in 1916, the area between Christ Church and Wood Quay occupied a crucial position as the focus of the traffic network for the whole south side of the city. The seeds of later developments may be found, however, in the remark that 'a fine site for a new building of good shape is provided [on this site], this would have formed an admirable Municipal Office if the Lord Edward Street site had not been already selected. A Bourse has now been suggested'. The appearance of any new building on the site was seen as important, for what are now familiar reasons: 'the regularly shaped building . . . should if possible, be kept low in order that the tower of Christ Church may be visible above it'.[2]

A preface to the volume, added in 1922 after the great destruction of the 1916 Rising and the Civil War in Central Dublin, drew attention to the many new sites then available: 'even the new Municipal Offices, for which land had been acquired in Lord Edward Street, might now be found a more convenient position on one of the demolished sites'.[3]

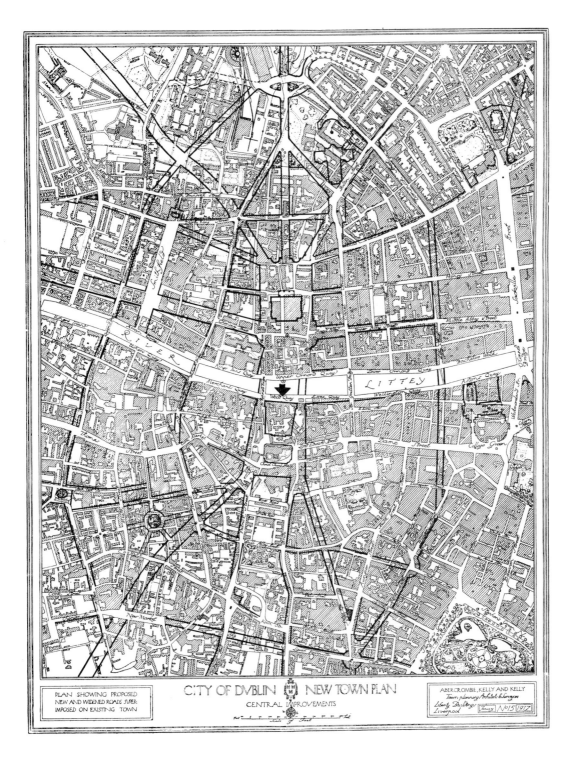

Abercrombie's radical road proposals, published 1922, showing (arrowed)
Wood Quay as a focal area for traffic in the city centre.

Little was done in the following twenty years to put any of the grandiose ideas of the Abercrombie plan for remodelling the city centre into practice, as the Council was mainly concerned with the task of re-housing. In the late 1930s, however, the need was felt again for a set of up-dated guidelines for the city's development and the same consultants were called in.

The outcome was the Abercrombie *Sketch Development Plan* for Dublin, published in 1941, which went back to the original proposal for a massive civic centre on the large block of land between Parliament Street, Lord Edward Street, Fishamble Street and Essex Quay, adjacent to City Hall. It was also specifically stated that: 'Our scheme provides for the opening of Christ Church Cathedral from the river. The grandeur of the structure standing on the hill is at present lost – blotted out by mean buildings'.[4] The Corporation's Town Planning Committee gave their approval of the site selected by the consultants for the new Civic Buildings, and added: '... in view of the inadequate and unsatisfactory accommodation in the existing scattered buildings used as civic offices, the Town Planning Committee agrees that new buildings are urgently necessary. It, therefore, recommends that steps be taken to invite designs for new municipal buildings by prize competition.'[5] In the following year 'the Corporation arranged to proceed with an *international competition* for designs for a new Municipal Headquarters, and appointed a body of architectural assessors to act as adjudicators'.[6]

This admirable but, in the circumstances of the time, surely over-ambitious proposal fell a victim to the 'Emergency', and the delay gave an opportunity for reassessment of the site. In due course it was realised that the preferred location, beside the City Hall, would be prohibitively expensive to acquire, as it contained a number of flourishing businesses, and so the adjacent block upstream, fronting onto Wood Quay, was adopted as an alternative site.[7]

THE ACQUISITION OF WOOD QUAY BY DUBLIN CORPORATION, 1951-1968

The area between Wood Quay and Christ Church, Winetavern Street and Fishamble Street had been in decline for some time. It was already largely in Corporation ownership and contained a cleansing yard, a coal yard and a waterworks depot among other amenities, though a number of private businesses and dwellings survived along the site perimeter, notably along Wood Quay itself. At the corner of Wood Quay and Winetavern Street stood the famous old pub, The Irish House, and there were a number of occupied houses along Winetavern Street and John's Lane. In 1951 the City Council adopted a report of the Finance and General Purposes Committee recommending the borrowing of the sum of £60,000 to erect civic offices at Winetavern Street.[8] By July 1955 Messrs Jones and Kelly, consulting architects, had prepared plans for a Civic Offices complex on the Wood Quay site:

> The central block facing the Quays consists of six storeys. The
> Winetavern Street and Fishamble Street frontages consist of five storeys,
> and the two front pavilions consist of four storeys. These offices, designed
> with a strong view towards utility and economy, will be constructed of
> reinforced concrete and faced with rustic bricks. The dressing throughout
> will be of limestone.

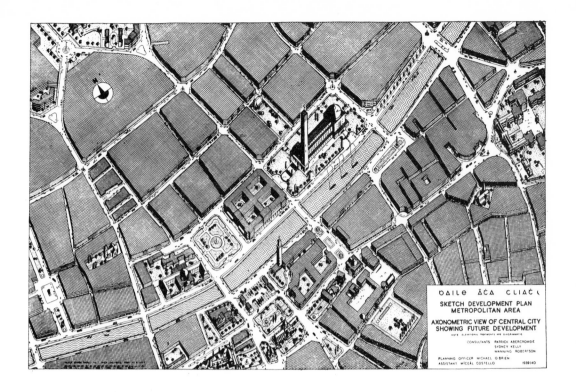

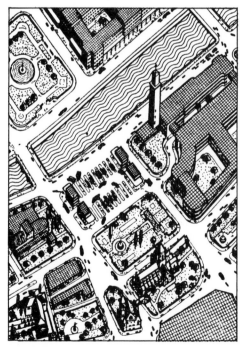

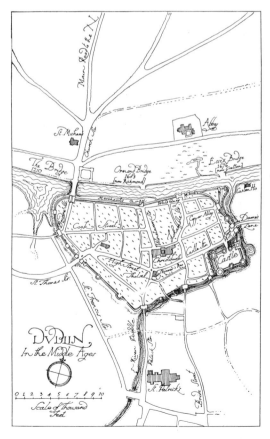

Top: Abercrombie's Sketch Development Plan, published 1941. Note the large civic centre development proposed for Wood Quay (detailed above).

Right: The area of medieval Dublin isolated by Abercrombie in his new town plan, published 1922.

The estimated cost of the whole project, to be build in four stages, was £680,000. The response of the Corporation's General Purposes Committee was dramatic: 'Plans approved, site to be cleared. . . . Tenders to be invited for piling'.[9]

A further obstacle to the erection of the Civic Offices arose in October 1955 when a deputation headed by the Dean of Christ Church Cathedral met the committee. The height of the office complex was the principal issue, and this was resolved at a meeting in November at which the Dean undertook to raise no further objections to the erection of the offices on the site in return for an offer from the committee to re-design the complex, lowering the principal block by one storey and the pent-house turrets by 20 feet.[10]

Later events were also foreshadowed by the contents of a letter from the City Manager to the General Purposes Committee: 'pointing out, *inter alia,* that at a recent meeting of U.C.D. Architectural Society statements were made that on one of the most wonderful sites in Dublin the Corporation were proposing to erect an early twentieth-century factory building and expressed the hope that this sad scheme would not be proceeded with; that apart from these hostile criticisms no support for the proposal had appeared in the public press'.[11]

Presumably in response to this 'hostile criticism' the City Council, at its next meeting, asked that the Committee report on the extra cost of providing a building in cut stone.[12] It proved impossible to proceed at this stage, however, because of legal difficulties over the use of compulsory powers for acquiring land for office building, and only after the passing of a special act of the Oireachtas in 1960 was the Corporation able to buy all the land it estimated was necessary.[13] This was done through the Winetavern Street/Wood Quay Area Compulsory Purchase (Provision of Civic Offices) Order of 1961, confirmed only in 1964 following a public enquiry, and the actual acquisition was not completed until 1968.

EMERGENCE OF ARCHAEOLOGICAL AWARENESS

While the Civic Offices Project was thus grinding its course through a maze of legal, political and bureaucratic obstacles, a revolution was taking place in the understanding of Dublin's history. In the 1950s it was still widely believed that the city of Dublin was built on a bog, an erroneous conclusion arrived at by Charles Haliday a century earlier and enshrined in his monumental standard work, *The Scandinavian Kingdom of Dublin.*[14] Numerous Viking and medieval objects had been recovered from street cuttings made for public utilities in the nineteenth century, but these were largely forgotten. 'Viking Dublin' was a concept related merely to occasional references in romantic tales and brief annalistic entries, and 'medieval Dublin' was scarcely more real outside the few surviving buildings and little-considered archival sources.

In 1961, however, the Office of Public Works began to undertake the rebuilding of the cross block at Dublin Castle and, following the demolition of the existing structure, the preparation of new foundations led to the discovery of earlier remains. The National Monuments branch of the Office of Public Works was called in, and soon it became clear that a find of remarkable importance had been stumbled upon. Beneath the interesting but not unexpected remains of the

Anglo-Norman castle, buildings of the pre-Norman city were recovered. For the first time modern archaeological techniques were applied to investigating Dublin's past, and with outstanding success. For a few weeks the newspapers were full of the exciting news, and a typed preliminary report was circulated in November 1962. Unfortunately the excavations were never completed, nor was any substantial report on them published, thus the full impact of the Dublin Castle excavations was never felt by the public, most of whom forgot the story with yesterday's newspaper.[15]

These excavations made their mark within academic circles, however, and the Dublin Castle discoveries were soon followed up by the National Museum who undertook excavations on a larger scale in 1962 and 1963 on a site at the corner of High Street and Nicholas Street, with similar results. It was now apparent to archaeologists, and others who took the trouble to familiarise themselves with the facts, that there was a good chance that a large area of central Dublin was underlain by deep and rich strata packed with infinite detail of the way of life of Dubliners since the foundation of the city, and this information could be recovered at the price of time and money. The size of the area was not then clear – nor is it yet known for certain – but it might be at least as large as the walled city of late medieval times, about forty acres (sixteen hectares), and larger if the extra-mural suburbs of Gaelic and Norman Dublin are included.[16]

As if to emphasise the prolific richness of underground Dublin, the National Museum resumed excavation in 1967 at a large site on High Street beside the old Tailor's Hall. Once again the deep, well-preserved layers of medieval remains were uncovered, giving new information about different crafts, building methods, town layout and every other topic of interest including human diet and fashion. All this was effecting a revolution in academic circles. It now became obvious, for example, that the modern city of Dublin was built, not on a bog, but on the dense, organic layers of packed vegetation and refuse created by the early inhabitants.

ARCHAEOLOGY VERSUS PLANNING, 1968-1977

But what effect was all this having on official planning and policy for the city? Apparently none at all. While the official archaeologists were laboriously discovering what lay beneath the city streets, the official planners were preparing to remove about ten per cent of the ground clear to bedrock inside the city walls without apparently being aware of any conflict of interest.

A few people, however, were aware and a little cold comfort can be gleaned from reading over the newspaper files of the 1960s and 1970s and realising that a great deal of the bitterness in the Wood Quay saga could have been avoided and a great deal of the needlessly sacrificed knowledge could have been recovered if communications had been better from the start. Has this lesson even yet been learned? The many wrangles over time extensions for the excavations at Fishamble Street during 1980 demonstrated that there was still no official appreciation in City Hall of the importance of archaeological excavation to any self-respecting historic city.

A single quotation will suffice to show that long before the ground was broken by the contractors at Wood Quay the archaeological implications of the civic offices project were clear. In a letter to the three Dublin dailies in November 1968,

P. Ó hÉailidhe listed a number of important buildings known to have stood on the site in medieval times, including Fyan's Castle, St Olaf's Church, the first Guildhall of the city and a length of the city wall, and stressed the importance of archaeological excavations being carried out in advance of site levelling and excavation for foundations. He concluded:

> The Corporation are, of course, well aware of this and, no doubt, will make adequate provision to ensure that excavation will not be carried out with heavy machinery until such time as the valuable evidence of the past has been fully recorded ... such a project may take years to complete, but it would be very much better for the Dublin Corporation to face this in the early stages than to wait until a contractor, tied up with agreements and bonds, should find that he is cutting his way through the pages of Dublin's history.[17]

Prophetic words!

The conflict of interest on the Wood Quay site thus predicted became a conflict in every sense of the word, largely because the significance of the archaeological discoveries in Dublin was not properly appreciated by more than a handful of people, very few of whom were in positions of authority or influence. The National Museum, as the organisation undertaking the excavations, had not used those excavations as an opportunity to educate the public in the nature or meaning of their discoveries, thus when the conflict came into the open the initial public reaction was composed largely of incomprehension and indifference. Only in 1977 was the public admitted for the first time to view the archaeological sites – then deserted for a year and under a thick carpet of weeds – and yet from that date the issue ceased to be an academic dispute and quickly became a popular campaign. This cannot be a coincidence.

The archaeological profession, too, was remarkably slow to take an active part in the issue , though clearly from the outset it was one of immense significance for Irish archaeology, both ethically and practically; later it became legally significant also, following the test case brought under the National Monuments Acts in 1978 and 1979. It is therefore unfair to apportion all blame to those promoting the Civic Offices when the contrary case was initially put forward so feebly. As destruction and outcry followed one another with sickening regularity between 1969 and 1979 it must surely have become obvious that mistakes had been made.

ARCHAEOLOGICAL EXCAVATIONS BEGIN AT WOOD QUAY

In late 1968, partly as a result of public pressure through the correspondence columns of the newspapers, the National Museum agreed to undertake some excavation on the Wood Quay site. However this was a site far larger than anything tackled before and it could obviously only be dealt with one piece at a time. The first area to be cleared of buildings was at the south-west corner of the site, between John's Lane and Winetavern Street, and the Museum began work there in January 1969. Meanwhile the Corporation had invited a number of developers to submit plans for the Civic Offices, and their various schemes were put on display. In July the Corporation's Board of Advisors short-listed two

vertical emphasis to facades ~ reinforcing existing character

B

C

Winetavern Street

wall of building fronting river

Above: Wood Quay frontage of the Civic Office complex as proposed in the _Architectural Review_, 1974.

Left: Vista from Wood Quay through the proposed Civic Office complex as envisaged by the _Architectural Review_, 1974. This design highlighted the Cathedral and harmonised with the scale of the surrounding buildings.

Below: The Stephenson & Gibney design which won the Civic Office competition in 1970. It disregards the existing quayside character and the townscape potential of the site.

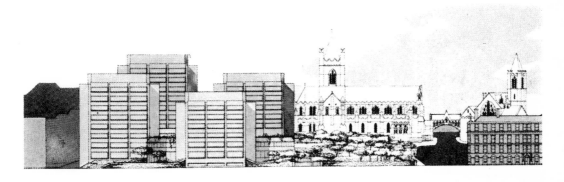

designs: the four-tower scheme of the Green Property Co. Ltd. (architects Stephenson, Gibney and Associates), a variant of which is now under construction, and a single twenty-storey tower proposed by Cramptons. Both were considered suitable by the advisors but the four-tower scheme was preferred on a majority vote; it was the cheaper, being costed at £2,833,844 in February 1970.[18]

At the end of the first season's excavations on Winetavern Street in October 1969 the press published accounts of the findings, including the discovery of the old city wall, and a percipient architect wrote in to say: 'If the work of building the Civic Offices gets under way inside twenty years the site will not have been fully investigated. . .'. In November at a seminar in Galway Martin Biddle, Director of the Winchester City Excavations, declared that: 'The redevelopment areas of the old walled city of Dublin offer an outstanding chance to investigate the origin and growth of the city. The opportunity will never recur'. He said that the existing project should be greatly augmented in funds and staff: 'This is a matter of international as well as national importance'.[19] This view has been more than confirmed by later discoveries but it is interesting to see the position clearly understood by independent observers so early on in the excavation of the site.

PLANNING PERMISSION GRANTED, 1970

During 1970 the Museum continued its excavations on the western perimeter of the site and the Corporation continued its negotiations with the developers. In November the Green Property Company, sponsors of the Stephenson design, were invited by Dublin Corporation to apply to the Corporation for planning permission, and this was granted on Christmas Eve. In spite of the awkward date appeals were lodged within the specified period, and an oral hearing was held in May 1971. That summer the National Museum completed investigation of its limited patch on Winetavern Street and concluded its work there 'within the walls'. Strangely, this careful and unhurried research project of three years duration was on a part of the site apparently never scheduled for any part of the four-tower complex, and was consequently one of the least threatened areas of the site.

To show that the site's interest was truly international, the Director of the National Museum of Denmark wrote to the Dublin city manager in January 1972 about

'. . . the Viking town which during recent years has been excavated in Dublin. This very momentous find has attracted attention all over Scandinavia . . . we are here very anxious to know whether you will try to preserve the old Viking town in Dublin so that it also in the future could be seen by people who are interested.'

This letter was passed to the writer's Irish counterpart, Dr A. T. Lucas, Director of the National Museum of Ireland, who replied that there was nothing either in settlement pattern or individual structures, which could be preserved, except for the old city wall.[20] The strange situation was thus created of outsiders requesting the care and preservation of what they claimed to be wonderful things, while those in immediate control insisted that there was nothing worthy or capable of preservation. This situation was repeated many times during the ensuing

A WARNING ON 'DIGS' IN DUBLIN

"He says they should be built somewhere else."

Left: An early warning of the archaeological significance of Wood Quay, *Evening Press*, 7 November 1969.

Evening Press reporter

There was no other national capital in Europe—and few towns of any kind—where the opportunities for archaeological research were so striking as in Dublin, the director of the Winchester Research Unit, Mr. Martin Biddle, said at a symposium at U.C.G.

Mr. Biddle warned the symposium, which was held on "The evolution of the Irish town: preservation and recording," that the Dublin opportunity would not long survive, due to the "catastrophic" destruction of early levels by most forms of modern construction.

matter of international as well as national importance." Mr. Biddle added.

A resolution passed at the annual general meeting of the Irish Economic Hostory Group supports Mr. Biddle's viewpoint.

It said: "That in view of the importance of archaeological excavation in the study and interpretation of the economic and social history of Irish towns and the City of Dublin in particular, this group urges the relevant authorities—the Corporation of Dublin, Department of Local Government and local authorities generally, An Foras Forbartha

decade. The record shows that on each occasion when the question was disputed, the claims of the site's archaeological importance were eventually recognised, usually by an extension of excavation time, but because those who contested the claims remained in control of the office development, it was always pushed ahead.

PLANNING PERMISSION CONFIRMED

In July 1972 the Minister for Local Government confirmed the grant of planning permission for the offices, subject to fifteen conditions. Shortly afterwards the Museum returned to the site for a brief investigation requesting permission to cut a long trench '. . . to test the stratification of the lower part of the site nearer the river. This could be expeditiously done by making a cut with a JCB. . . . You can take it that the work will be completed by February 1 1973'.[21]

In September the cost of the office scheme was estimated to have reached £5¼ million,[22] and by March 1973 the city manager reported that following the withdrawal of the Green Property Co., the Corporation were prepared to go ahead with the scheme, borrowing the money themselves.[23] This was approved by the City Council and the Minister during April, and with the money tied up matters quickly came to a head. In May the Corporation sent the National Museum notice to quit:

'I wish to advise that the site must be vacated by Mid-June as the consultant architects for the new Civic Offices project require possession of the whole site to arrange for the execution of preliminary demolition works. . .'.[24]

The Museum agreed and left.

This was the major watershed in the history of the site. Until July 1973 the site resembled many of the derelict areas of the old city, waste ground with empty buildings standing in decaying condition while legal and financial wrangles took place elsewhere. But the Museum excavations, carried on each summer since 1969 at the western perimeter, had shown that beneath the surface this was no ordinary building site but a place with very special potential for Dublin and for the history of Europe. In spite of this, the Corporation's archaeological adviser and agent, the National Museum of Ireland, had officially severed connection with the site which was now in the hands of demolition contractors. What followed was therefore inevitable.

SITE CLEARANCE BEGINS, 1973

The Wood Quay site at this time was sloping ground, involving a drop of 30 feet from John's Lane to Wood Quay. The first stage of preliminary site clearance was to demolish standing buildings, the next to level the site. This involved cutting a great wedge of ground out of the side of the hill to present a level area leading off Wood Quay, with a twenty-five foot 'cliff' at the back, below the old St John's graveyard. This clearance demonstrated that the whole site had had about 20 feet or more of archaeological deposits below the modern street level. It also exposed the top of the old city wall right across the site, continuing on from the piece found by the National Museum in 1969. Ironically it was while this major destruction of the site was taking place that the Museum opened its first exhibition of finds from the city excavations, 'Viking and Medieval Dublin', to coincide with the holding of the seventh Viking Congress in Dublin in August 1973.[25]

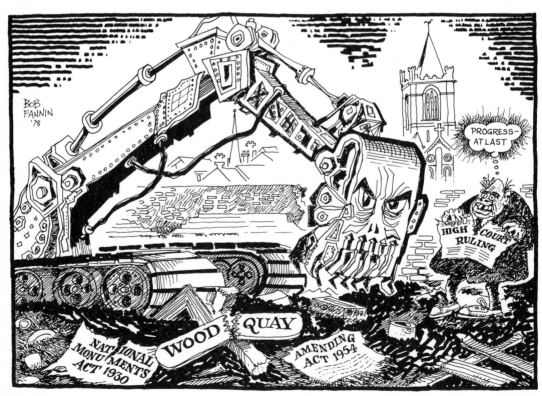

During the late summer and autumn of 1973 the public became aware for the first time that the clearance and levelling of the site, without any previous archaeological investigation of most of the area, was destroying valuable evidence. In November pressure built up against the National Museum, which was widely believed, even in official circles, to be still involved on the site. When a letter was sent to the Museum by the National Monuments Advisory Council about the damage to the city wall, the Director, Dr Lucas, took advantage of the opportunity to clarify the position: 'The Museum has completed its investigation of this site and has now no official connection with it', and he added: 'The Museum most emphatically does not wish to be associated with any strictures or adverse comments on the Corporation or its officers'.[26] This was at a time when scarcely five percent of the site had been investigated in any way. Dr Lucas also mentioned that the architects had been warned of the probability that further sections of the city wall would be uncovered during the clearance work, and that he had suggested they should discuss the matter with the Office of Public Works. A confirmation of the Museum's limited view of its role at this time is found in the minutes of a meeting held with the Corporation a week later, where the Director is recorded as saying that: 'The Museum is principally interested in the recovery and preservation of artifacts.' The Keeper of Irish Antiquities, Dr Joseph Raftery, agreed with this and added 'that the Museum would support the views expressed despite any reactions from less well informed sources'.[27]

The whole issue was now causing so much public controversy, however, that on 14 November a Government statement was issued halting development on the site and requesting the Corporation to examine possible alternative locations for the offices. In December the City Manager presented a report on five sites which had been examined. Only one, at Waterford Street, was considered suitable in all respects, and here the only argument against it was that a new design would be required, involving a delay of two years. The cost of the Wood Quay site would also have to be written off. It was also emphasised that the Director of the National Museum was quite satisfied for the existing scheme to go ahead.[28] Nevertheless, in January 1974, Mr Tully, the Minister for Local Government, told a delegation from the Corporation that the Wood Quay site should be kept as an open space because of '. . . its significant location in relation to Christ Church Cathedral, its archaeological importance and its value as an open space', and the Civic Offices would have to be built elsewhere.[29] This seemed like a final decision from the cabinet, but within three weeks the Minister had changed his mind. In February he wrote to the City Manager that the Government had reconsidered the matter and now felt that the Civic Offices should be built at Wood Quay after all. He accepted a new scheme put forward by the architects, relocating the four tower blocks to the eastern half of the site. The reasons for the reconsideration have never been given.[30]

This about-turn by the cabinet triggered off an intense period of public protest and lobbying, including an open meeting at the Mansion House addressed by well known archaeologists and others on 12 March 1974. Statements were issued by many organisations, including the Irish Association of Professional Archaeologists, calling for full excavation if the building was to go ahead. As the

Corporation came under increasing pressure to pay more heed to the archaeological implications of its plans, so it turned more and more to the National Museum to answer criticism. The Museum became totally identified with the Corporation line on the offices, and increasingly lost the confidence of professional colleagues. This became most clear at the time of the Wood Quay court cases in 1978-9, but the partnership was already fully formed by 1973-4. The spectacle of a national cultural and scientific institution actively co-operating in the destruction of outstanding evidence within its own special field of interest and responsibility made an indelible impression on thousands up and down the country and must have done the Museum itself incalculable harm. It has to some extent overshadowed the excellent work which the Museum has done in Dublin for many years from 1962 onwards.

THE EFFECTS OF PUBLIC OPINION

Another recurrent theme over the next few years was the demonstration that public pressure could influence policy on the site, not once but many times, but never sufficiently to make a permanent change of plan. On five or six occasions it was announced, or people got to know, that no more excavation would take place after a certain date, abandoning ever-decreasing unexcavated areas to the mercy of the contractors. The Museum regularly expressed its satisfaction at having completed its work, and yet public objection to the recommencement of bulldozing usually brought its eventual reward: the return of the Museum staff to the site, albeit after substantial destruction on each occasion.

We have already seen that it may only have been publicly expressed disquiet which got excavation under way on the site at all in 1969, and the second example of the influence of public opinion took place when the offices were relocated within the site and the whole scheme was almost called off. A third example was the initiating of excavation outside the old city wall, on the lower area of the site along Wood Quay, in the spring of 1974. A trial cut had been made in this area in 1972-3, but no arrangements for follow-up excavation were made. On the day following the Mansion House meeting a joint Corporation-Museum-Architects meeting was held, at which '. . . the Assistant City Manager repeated that the Corporation was prepared to accord to the Museum any facility on the site they required'.[31] As a result an agreement was drawn up dividing the proposed development area into four zones with a phased programme of excavation over three years. The Corporation issued a statement in relation to issues raised at the public meeting, saying that:

> . . . there was no need for concern about the future of the historic features
> of the Civic Offices site . . . every facility that the Museum had sought had
> been granted . . . The Corporation has also guaranteed that the area
> designated by the Museum authorities as one of prime archaeological
> importance on the site will not be built on for at least two years . . . By that
> time the Museum authorities estimated that they would have excavated
> all artifacts of archaeological importance on the site.[32]

Seven years later when excavations were still continuing the optimism of this

statement contrasted poorly with the view of the architect who went on record in 1969 that at least twenty years would be required.

The implication that areas *not* 'of prime archaeological importance' would be destroyed without full, or perhaps without any, archaeological excavation became the subject of strong comment, notably expressed by Ian Blake in his archaeological column in *The Irish Times* on several occasions.[33] The issue was raised in the Senate without apparent effect.[34] Nevertheless, in May 1974, the Museum recommenced excavation on the Wood Quay site after an absence of almost a year. The new director of excavations was Mr Pat Wallace, and his site was outside the old city wall, on the Area 1 of the site, reclaimed from the Liffey after the Norman conquest. This was the area *not* of 'prime archaeological importance' for which the Museum and Corporation had agreed that there should be unlimited access for archaeologists until July 1974, and limited access until March 1975, a remarkably short time for an area of over one acre and surely impossible to reconcile with the statement by the City manager, Matthew Macken, in October:

> He assured the members [of Dublin City Council] that the National Museum would excavate every spoonful of soil on the site and that the area would be fully excavated. All the fears being expressed were unfounded.[35]

Indeed fears were being widely expressed and by competent people well able to judge what was going on, in so far as they were able to get at the facts. In August An Taisce made public for the first time the existence of the four-phase timetable for Site 1 and emphasised its inadequacy: '. . . nothing short of a large scale emergency team can cope with the situation. International co-operation . . . should be sought immediately.'[36]

In September a group of university historians emphasised the same point and their letter provoked the first of a long series of editorial statements from all the national daily newspapers, calling for adequate treatment of national archaeological resources, which became one of the most striking and encouraging features of the whole Wood Quay campaign.[37]

CONSTRUCTION OF RETAINING WALL, 1974

In spite of a hitherto unprecedented public outcry the official machinery for the development of the site pressed forward relentlessly. On 25 September the Corporation accepted a tender of approximately £250,000 for preliminary site-work, including the construction of a retaining wall around the perimeter of the site. An An Taisce delegation was told by the architects that this would require the mechanical digging of a trench not more than 5 metres wide along the site border. In practice this trench was often three times as wide, sometimes more, and did great damage to all manner of archaeological evidence. In October the City Council debated the offices project in the light of the preliminary works tender, and decided to go ahead by a majority vote in spite of some objections. The Corporation decided to make a financial contribution to the archaeological excavations, for the first time, to help get them finished as quickly as possible.

In November 1974 the contradiction of attitudes became still more clear. On the one hand the Corporation announced revised time-tables for excavation on the site — in some cases shorter than before — and stated: '. . . the Museum authorities are satisfied that these time schedules will allow a complete and exhaustive search of the site for archaeological purposes'.[38] This included being out of Area 1 by 31 March 1975, where bulldozing was already taking place. On the other hand An Taisce predicted that the Museum would find itself presiding over an archaeological disaster unless it enormously increased its work force, by ten-fold if necessary.[39] In similar vein a letter was published by forty-one leading Irish academics, headed by the President of the Royal Irish Academy, calling for the establishment of a special unit to ensure the proper investigation of Dublin's past. This was a clear expression of mistrust in the Corporation-Museum control of the excavations.[40]

MEDIEVAL QUAYS DISCOVERED, 1975

During all this time, since excavations on site recommenced in May 1974, very few details of the work actually in progress on Wood Quay had reached the general public. In keeping with the policy adhered to since work in Dublin began, the excavations were strictly closed to visitors unless they were professionally involved. The Press was not encouraged, so that when in January 1975 it was announced that a 60-metre length of the wooden quay walls of medieval Dublin had been found, it was a revelation.[41] At once the question of an extension of time for the excavations was raised. By early March the question was clearly becoming acute, with only a few weeks left before the Museum was due to vacate Area 1 and no chance of the excavations being completed. Yet not only was no extension requested, but the Museum Director wrote to the Corporation:

We hope to finish our investigation of Area 1 of the Wood Quay site by the end of this month. We are completely satisfied that all significant data has been successfully retrieved and recorded to date and confidently expect to accomplish the same in the remaining fraction of the site within the time agreed upon.[42]

SIX-WEEK EXTENSION, 2 APRIL 1975

When the deadline arrived however, sufficient public agitation led to an apparent reprieve being granted, the first of the many 'six week extensions' offered to defuse the objections of people who were usually recommending six months or six years. So while the Museum was claiming that all work was completed to its entire satisfaction it was always able to continue working flat out, in this case employing sixty people on Area 1 alone, for as much time as could be obtained for it by the representations of third parties. It becomes clear in such circumstances that language was being misused by someone. The Corporation's claim that 'everything would be excavated to the last spoonful' was incorrect and should have read something like: 'everything that the Museum says it wants to excavate, or can get time to excavate, will be excavated', in other words the Museum can never have had, certainly not at the time we are discussing, a policy or programme of *complete* excavation of threatened areas, but only a *partial* objective. This was never admitted however, and so a good deal of confusion was caused. If the intention was to sample only, how was the decision made what to excavate and what to let go? This question has never been answered, or even usefully discussed, because until the policy of sampling was publicly acknowledged it could not even be asked. In these circumstances there will always be the suspicion that the decision was not taken on archaeological criteria, but on expedient factors relating to the office building schedule, and hence perhaps not taken by the archaeologists at all; at least not by the archaeologists as *archaeologists,* but perhaps by some of them in their role as obedient civil servants. Whether this was so or not in 1974-5 is a matter of conjecture but disclosures and statements made during the Wood Quay court cases in 1978 and 1979 make it clear that this was the form a few years later.

It was generally understood that the 'six week extension' announced on 2 April was to put back the bulldozing of Area 1 by this period, but it soon became obvious to observers that it was only a permission to the Museum to delay their departure from the area while the site was progressively demolished before their eyes.[43] Archaeologists were seen to be working within feet of heavy bulk excavators, in considerable physical danger, and unofficially the site director was under severe pressure from the developers to get off the site as quickly as possible, and not to raise objections to the demolition of archaeological structures. In spite of this, invaluable evidence of an impressive series of wooden quays was uncovered – in some cases to be seen for a few hours only – extending dry land by stages from the old town wall out to the modern line of the quays. In and around these quays were found the remains of many wooden boats of about the twelfth century, the most extensive group of this period known to survive in Western Europe. It is a source of pride to those involved that so much was recovered when official policy had been against any excavation in this area, mingled with regret that so much was destroyed unrecorded.[44] The official view can be found in a statement by Dr Joseph Raftery, Keeper of the Irish Antiquities at the National Museum, given to the Corporation in April. Characterising the ancient structures at Wood Quay as 'a few inches of wattle', he said of their preservation: '. . . uninformed lay persons require that this be done . . . the motives of people pressing for it may be questioned'.[45]

EXTENSION EXTENDED, 25 APRIL 1975

On 9 April a special meeting of Dublin City Council was told by the Director and Keeper of Irish Antiquities at the Museum that they were satisfied with the archaeological excavation programme, and that the area was being investigated totally, in spite of overwhelming evidence to the contrary.[46] Once again public protest was directed towards obtaining proper archaeological conditions on the site, and demands for an independent inquiry were frequent. On 25 April Dr Raftery stated that the Corporation's extension for Area 1 was now 'open-ended': it would be used to excavate 'as quickly as we possibly can'.[47]

An independent report prepared for Professor Dudley Edwards of U.C.D. by an (anonymous) insider familiar with the site confirmed that, even with this new extension, all was not well:

1 The new (open-ended) time extension is yet another indication of the piece-meal attitude of the National Museum. If the extension had been arranged at the beginning of April, when the six weeks extension was announced, there would have been no need for the hurried removal of some of the most important features of the site. In other words the extension is too late. At least half of Area 1 has already been cleared by the mechanical digger of the contractors.
2 The time extension applies only to the area currently under excavation . . . the construction works of the contractors, outside this area, have revealed several medieval structures. The mechanical digger is still working in these areas'.[48]

To emphasise the nature of the spoil being removed by the machines, the tip-head at Ringsend became a hunting ground for collectors of Viking and medieval objects, and even solid oak beams of medieval structures.[49] This was, of course, subsequently repeated, as was the intervention of overseas archaeological experts. For example, in June 1975, An Taoiseach Liam Cosgrave received a telegram from the Director of the Council for British Archaeology describing the Wood Quay excavations as 'of European importance yielding results unparallelled elsewhere', and ending:

The C.B.A. earnestly entreats [the] Irish Government['s] immediate intervention to prevent destruction of this irreplaceable site before proper archaeological excavation [is] completed'.[50]

In July a second team from the National Museum under Breandán Ó Ríordáin began excavations on Area 2 of the site, the Viking area within the old city wall along Fishamble Street; the deadline agreed by the Corporation and Museum for this area was originally March 1976, later reduced to December 1975. It is

Thirteenth-century ship timbers in the course of excavation at Wood Quay.

interesting to realise that after much more excavation, and much more unsupervised destruction, this area was still being worked in March 1981, when the excavations concluded.

A YEAR OF INDECISION, 1975

The impression created by these events of 1975 is that the Corporation was at last beginning to realise the difficulty of its position. It had been possible for the councillors to believe up to this time, with a few notable exceptions, that the Corporation really was doing its best by giving the National Museum *carte blanche,* and that they could press on with the building plans as well as getting a full excavation done by the Museum. Few councillors had personal knowledge of the site excavation before this date, and the officials and architects who may have realised the inconsistencies did nothing to put forward facts or even doubts which would in any way hinder the office construction programme.

The most obvious responsibility for allowing the building project to continue, to the ultimate disadvantage of all parties, falls on the senior policy-making officials of the National Museum. They continued to tell the Corporation what they wanted to hear, that they would be out of the site by whatever happened to be the current deadline, and then to represent this period as exactly the time needed to do a complete and total excavation to first class standards of the area in question. It was left to third parties, time and again, to show up the inconsistencies of these assurances. The reaction by the Museum acting as the Corporation advisers was always the same: to deny that more time was needed, to try and discredit the claims of the third parties by personal attacks on their competence and motives, and then to prove their opponents' case over and over again by continuing to excavate for whatever period of an extension had been obtained for them.

It may be asked what other options were open to the Museum. Were they not attempting to maintain good faith with the local authority by settling for the best deal possible and then holding to it, but subsequently taking advantage of any extension which was offered? This explanation would cover many of the facts but not all. It could have been admitted, which was the fact, that total archaeological excavation of such a large, complex site was not possible for the Museum with its existing resources, within anything like the time scale which was available. Then either a programme of sampling could have been proposed, or other institutions could have been asked to help, or the Corporation could have been advised that the whole project was impossible. It was the Museum which could and should have made the assessment of the situation that would have thrown up these options and it is in fact almost inconceivable that the staff concerned should not have done so privately. But by continuing to back up the Corporation officially with advice which could no longer be supported by their colleagues, they allowed the Corporation to blunder forward to an untenable position.

In the years since 1975 we have seen an evolution of opinion within the Dublin City Council from a position where the official line on the offices was held by an overwhelming majority to that following the 1979 local elections when a majority was consistently trying to revoke the contract, and was restrained only by technical impediments.

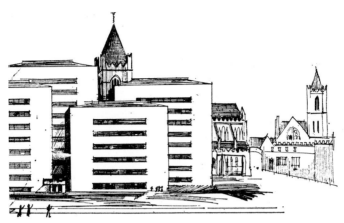

"Far from destroying the view of Christ Church Cathderal, the Corporation project has enhanced it."—Noel Carroll (28-3-'79).

Drawing of four towers of the proposed Civic Office complex, from *The Irish Times,* 4 April 1979, compared with a photograph of the two towers under construction in 1982. Corporation spokesmen maintained that the view of Christ Church from the quays would not be obscured.

Work proceeded on the Museum excavations for the remainder of 1975, except when the allocated money ran out just before Christmas. All the workmen were put on one week's notice, but trades union representation managed to get extra funds before work had to stop.[51] Early in 1976 there were indications that the Corporation was running into financial problems with the funding of the Civic Office project. In March the Museum was offered a three-month extension for work on Area 2, and this was accepted.[52] In May a Corporation spokesman stated that he was unable to say when the Civic Offices would be built. It was then estimated that the total cost of the scheme would be £12 million, with an extra £2 million for every two years delay.[53] On the last day of June the Corporation once more wrote to the Museum Director offering a further extension in Area 2, until the end of November. This however, was turned down, and Dr Lucas replied: 'We will not be taking advantage of your offer as the excavations (on the Wood Quay site) have been terminated, and we are, at the moment, in the process of withdrawing from the site'.[54] This withdrawal was effected by the end of July 1976 and no more archaeological excavation took place on the site until December 1977, eighteen months later.

The reason for this Museum refusal to continue remained a mystery until, during the High Court action of June 1978, correspondence between the Museum and the Corporation preceeding the exchange quoted above was 'discovered'. On the face of it, it would seem ideal to have a lengthy period for excavation on the site without the ever-present pressure from the offices construction timetable, under the strain of which all work since 1974 had been carried out. It was revealed however that following a series of demands for the payment of a sum of £5,000 for the removal of spoil earlier in the year, the Corporation threatened the Museum on 28 June with legal proceedings if the bill was not met. A week later the Museum felt obliged to decline the preferred extension.[55]

From July 1976 the Wood Quay site entered a strange twilight period, in which for over a year it joined the great number of derelict sites in Dublin. Weeds grew in the archaeologists' trenches and vandals raided the site and made a bonfire of the abandoned excavation huts and the piles of medieval timbers which had been kept in the forlorn hope that someone might one day find some secure place to store them.

The usual protests were forcefully made, in particular the point that a skilled team built up over a couple of years was being disbanded; furthermore, no one was retained to work towards the eventual publication of the results. But although a return to excavation could generally be secured when the alternative was visible destruction, the present alternative of gentle delay and decay was insufficiently dramatic to lead to any action. And yet it was plain that a very good opportunity was being missed and the fact of eighteen months of inaction was repeatedly cited later as evidence that the Museum's statement that 'excavations have been terminated' meant that total excavation had been completed.

The Wood Quay saga thus entered a new phase, with repeated appeals to the courts to protect the archaeological remains as a National Monument, a part of the saga told by Fr Martin himself.

'What the Irish do to their national treasures.

CHAPTER 2

F. X. MARTIN osa

Politics, Public Protest and the Law

On 8 April 1976, a number of people in Dublin – representing archaeology, medieval history, historical geography, architecture, town planning, local history, as well as city aldermen – met and formed a new association, the Friends of Medieval Dublin. Their object was to foster by every available means an appreciation of the medieval Dublin heritage. Realising that this was not possible without an accurate knowledge of the medieval city, it was decided to publish what had hitherto been lacking, maps of medieval Dublin, including one which represents medieval Dublin superimposed on the background of the modern city. For the first time it was possible for city planners and developers to have an accurate picture of the most sensitive archaeological and historical area of the city. It came at the eleventh hour. The Dublin Corporation was near to signing a contract for the building of civic offices at Wood Quay.

The Friends of Medieval Dublin, realising that time was running out for the Viking site upon which the civic office complex was to be built, proposed to Dublin Corporation that guided tours of the site, at Wood Quay, be organised during the summer months of 1977. Permission was readily given by the Corporation, as well as money for minor expenses. The success of the tours, conducted each week-end from July to October can be judged by the calculation that 12,000–15,000 people participated. The harmonious atmosphere was disrupted in late July when it was established by the Friends that one part of the site, as yet unexcavated archaeologically, was due to be mechanically removed in the autumn.

This very urgent problem was the subject of a discussion at City Hall on 4 August 1977, when representatives of the Friends and of the Dublin Civic Group met Corporation officials and the architects of the proposed civic offices. The vague assurance by the architects that the machines would stop if objects of archaeological value were discovered had no ring of conviction and the preservationists failed to convince Corporation officials that the signing of the building contract should be postponed. In order to alert the public as to what was at stake a public meeting, organised by the Friends, was held in the Mansion House on 4 October. An overflow audience vehemently expressed its opposition to the building of the civic offices until the site had been scientifically excavated. An appeal to the Minister for Education, Mr John Wilson, produced results. He announced on 7 October that there would be a stay-of-execution at Wood Quay

Wood Quay site called 'this hole in Dublin' by Cork professor

THE head of the Department of Archaeology at University College, Cork, Professor Michael J. Kelly, giving evidence in the Wood Quay case in the High Court, Dublin yesterday, said that money spent on other places would give a vastly better bird's eye view of medieval Ireland and this money would be far better employed doing that than spending it all on "this hole in Dublin."

Newspaper report of the court proceedings, 30 June 1978.

Legal history being made: Mr Justice Hamilton visits the scene of the action, 30 June 1978.

for six months, and that money would be made available for an archaeological team to work there.

Fears were dispelled for the time being, and archaeologists, under the direction of the National Museum, began work on the site. The alarm bells rang once again, but this time with greater urgency, when workmen on the site – and that in itself is significant – sent word to the Friends that the bulldozers had orders to move in on the unexcavated part of the site and destroy the Viking earthen defence banks, over 1,000 years old, after the lunch-break on Monday, 28 November 1977. The banks, of great international archaeological interest and value, were to be the immediate object of attack. However, much more was at risk since the proposed destruction represented the ruthless method by which the Corporation officials intended to deal with the remaining Viking and medieval evidence. To stop them was a race against time, with a mere half a day to produce an answer. The only effective answer was the law – a High Court injunction to restrain the bulldozers – but this required an expert legal team. Against the odds of time and circumstances, a talented legal trio made themselves available: Mr Donal Barrington, now Mr Justice Barrington of the High Court, as Senior Counsel; Senator Mary Robinson as Junior Counsel; and Mr Nicholas Robinson as Solicitor.

The case was opened on 28 November before Mr Justice Declan Costello of the High Court and a temporary injunction was granted. A lengthy legal process ensued, with unavailing appeals to the Corporation and to the Commissioners of Public Works to state if the area in question was a National Monument. The Attorney General, Mr Anthony Hederman, agreed to join with Professor Martin in prosecuting the case. There was a change of judge, with Mr Justice Liam Hamilton replacing Mr Justice Costello, and the defenders of Wood Quay were fortunate enough to add Mr Thomas C. Smyth, S.C., to their legal team.

The trial of the action, which took place finally on 28-30 June 1978, was a high point of interest not only for archaeologists and scholars but for the general public. The drama of the situation was accentuated by the fact that, while the trial was taking place in the Four Courts, the site in dispute, Wood Quay, was in view across the river Liffey, within less than five minutes walking distance. The massive cranes, temporarily inactive, stood sharply in contrast against the background of Christ Church Cathedral.

Many local and international experts gave evidence on behalf of Wood Quay. Dublin Corporation called three archaeologists to give evidence on their side: Dr Joseph Raftery, the then Director of the National Museum; Mr Etienne Rynne of University College Galway, who, it was later revealed, was an official consultant to the Corporation, and Professor Michael O'Kelly of University College Cork, who made a memorable statement from the witness box describing the Wood Quay site as 'this hole in the ground' in Dublin. When cross-examined about his statement Professor O'Kelly declared that Dublin archaeologists had so described *his* excavations in Cork!

Before Mr Justice Hamilton gave judgement on 30 June he went on a tour of the Wood Quay site. His conclusion was incisive:

I have carefully considered the evidence in this matter and I have found the evidence of the plaintiff [Fr Martin] and the witnesses called on his behalf to be coercive. They have satisfied me that it is of national importance that the site of Wood Quay, which is the subject of these proceedings, between the City Wall, Fishamble Street, John's Lane and Winetavern Street should be preserved.

Thus, the Wood Quay site was declared to be a National Monument, the first to be so specified by a legal process since the foundation of the Irish Free State in 1922.

There was universal acclaim for Mr Justice Hamilton's judgement. The leader writers of the three national daily newspapers greeted it as a commonsense and enlightened decision. The hope that it would not be challenged on appeal was expressed, but an underlying unease was also apparent. The *Irish Independent* leader writer did not disguise scepticism about the Corporation's acceptance of the court judgement:

Now, thanks to the persevering efforts of a few dedicated men and women, the site has been given a new lease of life. Or has it? Will the Corporation find some legal way round the High Court's decision and continue with the building plans? It would be flying in the face of reason to do so.

Reason does not always rule in the Dublin Corporation offices, nor did it on this occasion.

The doubts and fears expressed were only too well founded as events were soon to prove. It was announced within a matter of days that Dublin Corporation had requested the Commissioners of Public Works to join with them in giving consent to demolish and remove wholly the National Monument. There was a blithe disregard for the national cultural heritage and for the will of the people.

LOOPHOLES

Section 14 of the National Monuments Act of 1930 declares that it shall not be lawful for any person to demolish, remove or injure in any way a National Monument, or even to dig or plough the ground in its proximity; but then it adds an escape clause, sub-section (3), which allows for permission to demolish. This can be given, as a joint consent, by the Commissioners of Public Works (the official custodians of all such National Monuments) and the local authority (in this case Dublin Corporation). For what reasons? The sub-section goes on to say:

The Commissioners and every local authority are hereby respectively authorised to give such consent as is mentioned in the foregoing sub-section if and whenever they think it expedient in the interests of archaeology or for any other reason so to do and are hereby authorised to attach to any such consent all such conditions and restrictions as they think fit.

The common assumption, certainly that of the Friends, was that the unlimited and all-important clause, 'for any other reason', was designed to cover extraórdinary circumstances in which health, public safety or national security were in question, not a building programme in everyday circumstances.

News that the Corporation, if given the consent of the Commissioners, intended to proceed with the demolition of the National Monument set off a public reaction which was quick, hot, and heavy. The newspapers reflected the general exasperation, and representative bodies likewise expressed their convictions in public statements. At this point the Government intervened with a temporary compromise to meet the popular outcry. Mr Pearse Wyse, Minister of State at the Department of Finance (under which the commissioners of Public Works operate), announced on 25 August 1978 that excavations at Wood Quay should continue for 'a period of not more than six weeks. . . . When the excavation is completed, unless some new archaeological find of great importance has been made, the Corporation will be granted permission to proceed with the building of the Civic Offices'. The official attempt, through Mr Wyse's statement, to stem the rising wave of protest was as effectual as King Canute's command that the sea stop at his throne.

MANSION HOUSE PROTEST: SEPTEMBER 1978

Public indignation at the thought that authorisation for the destruction of the Viking remains was seriously contemplated rose rapidly and was canalised by the Friends of Medieval Dublin. It found an outlet on the evening of 14 September when over 2,000 people crammed into the Mansion House, along the passageways, up on to the platform and out on to Dawson Street. When the official speakers had finished a number of resolutions were adopted by acclamation from the crowd: no buildings on the National Monument site; no high-rise buildings on any part of the Wood Quay site; re-locate and build the proposed offices as an urgent priority; inform the Minister for Finance, Mr George Colley, that the National Monument must be preserved. As immediate practical measures it was decided to lobby TDs and city councillors; to mount a massive campaign of signed petitions addressed to George Colley, as the cabinet minister responsible for Wood Quay; and to organise a Viking march from Leinster House to Wood Quay on 23 September.

The last part of the meeting was given to speakers from the floor, and, though these had necessarily to be limited in number and chosen at random, they represented a complete cross-section of Irish society; their spontaneous and vividly expressed sentiments conveyed the electric atmosphere of the assembly. Two of the memorable speakers from the floor were Denis Larkin, the veteran trade union leader, and Maeve Durkan, a thirteen-year-old schoolgirl.

But Wood Quay was not just a Dublin affair. On the evening of 22 September it was the topic of discussion on the RTE current affairs programme 'Frontline', with two teams participating: representatives of the Corporation and of those defending Wood Quay. The television reviewers in the newspapers and journals agreed that the honours went easily to the defenders of the National Monument. The programme was a timely curtain-raiser for the Viking march due to take place the next day.

The Danish flag flies from Casey's house in Fishamble Street, overlooking Wood Quay, marking the visit to Dublin of Queen Margarethe of Denmark. Her request to visit the excavations was turned down.

A Dubliner prepared to defend his heritage.

While the protesters assemble, discussions take place betwen Fr F. X. Martin, Maurice Craig, Nick Robinson and Senator Mary Robinson.

The first Viking march moves off from Kildare Street, 23 September 1978.

Professor Michael Herity lays a symbolic wreath at the door of the
Commissioners of Public Works, St Stephens Green, during the
Viking march.

The marchers converging on Christ Church Cathedral with the
Wood Quay site on the left.

On the eve of the Viking March the Friends of Medieval Dublin received two important messages of support. The National Council of Muintir na Tíre, representative of rural Ireland, called for the preservation of Wood Quay and for the re-location of the proposed civic offices; the weight of the trade union movement was also thrown in as support when leaders of the Irish Congress of Trade Unions and of two of the biggest unions in the country, the ITGWU (Irish Transport and General Workers Union) and WUI (Workers Union of Ireland), sent a joint telegram to the Taoiseach, Mr Jack Lynch, calling for the preservation of the National Monument because of its 'enormous importance for the social history of the Irish people and its place as part of our national heritage'.

On the morning of the march, the first leader of *The Irish Times* was entitled 'Save it!', and spelled out what was at stake:

> The unique and international importance of the Viking site is part of what makes the Wood Quay case different. More important, perhaps, is the realisation that the final decision to build on the site was taken against expert advice, coming not through outside lobbies or pressure groups, but through the official mechanism designed to provide that advice (The National Monuments Advisory Council); and, also, of course, in the light of a High Court designation of Wood Quay as a National Monument. The decision has all the appearance of a deliberate and brutal opting for the uncouth, for the short-term, and to hell with heritage, history and higher values.

It would be accurate to describe the march as one of the memorable demonstrations in recent Irish history. It was unique because it embraced all classes, creeds, cultural interests and political groups. The trade unions were there with their banners, as were the Irish Hotels Federation and Dublin Tourism. The site workers marched as a group under their own banner, as did Conradh na Gaeilge with the slogan *'Cosain an Ché'*. The eminent historian, Dr F. S. L. Lyons, Provost of Trinity College, marched with other academics from both the National University of Ireland and Trinity College, Dublin. One of the most heartening sights was the number of school children, identified by their school banners and accompanied by their teachers.

Dublin went festive for the occasion. The march was led by the resounding music of the ITGWU band, followed by city councillors and aldermen in their blue-green-yellow robes and tricorn hats; academics in their varied and vivid robes; adults and children in Viking costumes; groups with placards and banners. The march moved at a smart pace from Leinster House, halting to leave a letter of protest at the National Museum, a petition at Government Buildings, a funeral wreath at the offices of the Commissioners of Public Works in St Stephen's Green, then continued on by Grafton Street and College Green to leave another letter of protest and wreath at City Hall, and so to Christ Church, Wood Quay, and the final rousing speeches. It was the biggest march in Dublin since the workers came out in the Great Strike of 1913, said Denis Larkin; even bigger than the anti-apartheid march of 1970, said Niall Greene of the Labour Party. One police estimate put the number at 17,800, with television cameras showing the head of the march at Christ Church while the tail was still at the top of Grafton Street; and over 1,000 older sympathisers remained as onlookers in St Stephen's Green and its vicinity. Around 20,000 was the accepted figure. Olivia O'Leary of *The Irish Times* succinctly commented, 'the City of Dublin had found a cause'.

The Cabinet got the message. When it met on 26 September, for the first session since the summer recess, Wood Quay was a top priority. The Government issued a formal statement on the problem but made no mention of the essential fact that a joint consent, of 29 August, to demolish the National Monument was already in existence. Instead, it declared that 'the Government have directed that the Commissioners of Public Works should consent to an extension of time to complete further investigation of the site'. No time limit was set for the investigation, but neither was there mention of preservation, a main object of the defenders of Wood Quay. In hard political terms no more than a breathing space was being allowed, though this stay of execution was in itself a major victory. Further, some two weeks later, on 16 October, as we shall see soon, an all-important statement was made by the Commissioners of Public Works, specifying that no final decision had yet been taken on the future of the Wood Quay site. This was a honeyed lie, designed to gull a credulous public. Only those in the know, the Commissioners and the senior officials of the Corporation, were aware of the deception.

PRESS CLIPPINGS

Rarely has the media so clearly and consistently reflected public concern. As far back as 6 February 1978, *The Irish Times* weekly poetry competition had been devoted to 'Lines upon Wood Quay'. Among the entries printed was one by Liam Brophy entitled 'The Wood Quay Wreckers' and with the following opening verse:

O Swift, thou should'st be living at this hour —
Ireland hath need of thee and thy sharp pen
To lacerate the Lilliputian men
Who tie us with red tapes of petty power.

John Healy of *The Irish Times,* one of the most influential columnists in the country, used his sharp pen as a lethal lance on behalf of Wood Quay. Three successive articles of his rivetted public attention on the problem: 'In praise of gentle anarchy' (11 September 1978), 'Jack can save Wood Quay' (25 September), and 'The politics of Wood Quay' (30 September).

Hibernia, a lively weekly national review, ran two successive issues with Wood Quay as the front-page story. On 21 September, its cover carried black and red banner headlines, 'Exclusive – Wood Quay; Secret Report Revealed'. Inside, it carried the confidential report of the National Monuments Advisory Council which revealed that Pearse Wyse, the Minister of State, had completely misrepresented their views when he implied in a public statement that the members of the Council supported his consent to the destruction of the National Monument. The opposite was the truth, as the confidential report demonstrated.

On the following week the front page of *Hibernia* was an ingenious montage of

FRIENDS OF MEDIEVAL DUBLIN

Save our National Monument at Wood Quay

PUBLIC MEETING

"WOOD QUAY – A EUROPEAN HERITAGE"

MANSION HOUSE

Thursday, March 29th

at 7.30 p.m.

Admission Free

Chairman: **Rev. Prof. F. X. Martin**

Main Speaker: **Dr. Henrik Jansen**
(Svenborg Museum, Denmark)

WOOD QUAY RALLY & MARCH

Saturday, March 31st

at 11.00 a.m.

Assembly Point:

Leinster House

Martyn Turner's cartoon depicting Lord Mayor Paddy Belton actively encouraging the demolition of Wood Quay while the Taoiseach, Jack Lynch, and judiciary stand idly by (left).

prominent personalities photographed during the Viking march of 23 September. The main article, by editor John Mulcahy, was entitled 'The Politics of Wood Quay', and the leading article, headed 'Early Warning Signal', spoke more prophetically than it could have realised:

> It was untypical of Fianna Fáil to be caught out so badly over Wood Quay. The Party of Reality prides itself on the sensitivity of its political antennae, and rightly so. . . . How then could it be so badly out of touch on an issue which – as last Saturday's massive demonstration amply illustrated – aggravated so many citizens of the capital city? . . . The Coalition gravely underestimated the new sophistication of the Irish electorate and paid the price. Fianna Fáil would be well advised to interpret the Wood Quay demo as an early warning signal to avoid the same pitfall.

How widespread was the support for Wood Quay was made manifest from two unexpected sources. *An Phoblacht,* in its issue of 30 September, gave front-page coverage to Wood Quay with a photograph captioned 'Street politics in Dublin', as well as a special article, and the leading article entitled 'Wood Quay barbarism is so very much in Leinster House character'. *Hot Press,* the weekly 'pop' music magazine, in the issue of early October, cried aloud its defiance of bureaucracy and blind government in the main article, 'Wood Quay – a Pyrrhic Victory'. This same support from unexpected quarters continued. It had already been shown, for example, when Con Houlihan, perhaps the best-known of the national sports writers, devoted his column in the *Evening Press* of 9 March 1978 to Wood Quay. It was repeated when the editors of nine leading Irish Catholic magazines signed a joint letter of appeal on behalf of Wood Quay, published in the newspapers on 22 September 1978.

All this support was not merely a Dublin phenomenon. Frank Kilfeather, in his review of provincial papers in *The Irish Times* of 2 October 1978, headed his feature 'Country-wide interest evinced in Wood Quay', and cited the leader-writers of papers such as the *Nationalist* of Carlow and the *Donegal Democrat* as advocates of Wood Quay. At a different, but important, level was the nation-wide interest shown on behalf of the youth of the country by two articles on Wood Quay, which appeared in December 1977 and November 1978 in *Young Citizen,* the monthly magazine published for schools by the Institute of Public Administration.

One of the most impressive manifestations of popular support for Wood Quay was the almost unbroken succession of 'Letters to the Editor' in the three national daily newspapers. At moments of crisis, it became a positive barrage of correspondence, and ninety-nine per cent of the writers were in favour of preserving the National Monument. The letters came from cultural societies, residents' associations, teachers' organisations, trade unions, scholars at home and abroad, individual citizens, and school children.

RESIDENTS, UNIONS, POLITICIANS

Employees of Dublin Corporation were the one solid group who reacted unfavourably to any delay in the building programme for the civic office complex. They would be there a mere 35-40 hours per week, 48 weeks a year. The people of the area represented by the Liberties Association, however, would have to live with the four fortress-like tower blocks 24 hours a day, 7 days a week, 365 days a year. Doubtless, it was the democratic reason of priority for those living in the Liberties area, as against those who would be working there, which decided both the major trade unions and the Labour Party to come to the support of Wood Quay.

The policy document issued by the Labour Party, on 2 October 1978, was the first considered stand on the Viking site taken by any one of the main political parties, and for this alone it deserves credit. It was a compromise which, while proposing that there be no building on the National Monument site, allowed for the re-location and re-design of the offices on a part of the Wood Quay site which had been bulldozed and was of little use to the archaeologists or historians. Thus, while the National Monument site would be saved, the view of Christ Church would not be obscured and some substantial office accommodation would be provided for the Corporation employees. The following day, though not directly connected with the Labour Party proposal, there was a motion in the City Council, supported by the Community Councillors, to have the civic offices re-located on the north side of the city. This was defeated by 28 votes to 8.

The behaviour of the Government at this stage did not clarify the situation. After the Viking march of 23 September, the Government had issued a statement saying it had 'directed that the Commissioners of Public Works should consent to an extension of time to complete further investigation of the site'. It thus emerged that the Government was the ultimate judge in the matter; nevertheless it gave no length of time for the investigation nor did it guarantee to preserve the Viking and medieval remains on the site. The controversy continued to rage and, on 16 October, the Commissioners of Public Works announced a further two months of investigation of Wood Quay, *'pending a final decision on the future of the [National] Monument'.* All looked to the Government to make a pronouncement.

Evidence, which should have been considered irresistible, continued to accumulate in favour of Wood Quay. The National Monuments Advisory Council, the official advisory body of archaeological experts to advise the Government, followed its recommendations of September 1978 with even stronger recommendations in November and December. Equally strong recommendations came from An Taisce, the official conservation body in the country. The Committee on Culture and Education of the Council of Europe, which had already sent several messages of concern to the Irish Government and to Dublin Corporation, despatched a strongly worded telegram, on 6 December, to the Taoiseach, Mr Jack Lynch, and to Mr Pearse Wyse.

Though all these appeals fell on culturally deaf ears in Irish Government circles, there were responsible Irish political figures who made a major effort to bring home to the Government that part of the national cultural heritage was at risk. The Council of Europe telegram arrived in Dublin on the very day, 6 December, that a formal debate was opened in the Senate on the motion:

> That Seanad Éireann calls on the Government to make an order to preserve indefinitely the Viking site at Wood Quay, already designated a National Monument, in view of the many other sites available in Dublin for civic offices.

MINISTER FOR FINANCE

BOB FANNIN

'You've just missed Mr Colley — he dashed out to a protest march.'

The proposers were three of the university representatives, Senators Augustine Martin, Timothy Trevor West and Gemma Hussey. Senator Martin had made a notable speech in the chamber, on behalf of Wood Quay, as far back as October 1974. Though the Government now called in all its forces, including its two representatives at the European Parliament, Ruairí Brugha and Michael Yeats, the motion was defeated by only one vote. Two facts are worthy of record at this point. A university representative and professional historian, Professor J. A. Murphy of University College Cork, voted for the destruction of the National Monument, whereas two of the Government nominees, Senators Ken Whitaker and Gordon Lambert, voted for Wood Quay.

At no stage was it revealed by Minister of State Pearse Wyse that a joint consent, between the Commissioners of Public Works and Dublin Corporation, had been sealed as far back as 29 August. The Government must, or should, have known that the decision had already been taken and formally committed to writing on 29 August. This was, at the worst, official deception, at the least, official bungling. Nothing less.

The Senate, as well as the public, were led to believe that no final decision had yet been taken by the Government, and that the final decision about the fate of Wood Quay rested with the Government. This had been expressly stated by Mr Wyse on 10 October 1978, and again on 7 December, when he addressed the Senate. It was re-affirmed on 14 December when he announced that he was seeking the further views of the National Monuments Advisory Council 'before making his final recommendations to the Government'. The same assumption underlay a motion and lively debate which took place in the Dublin City Council on 11 December. Despite the sleet, hundreds of citizens had on that occasion gathered outside the City Hall with placards to manifest their intense interest in the motion. By a curious coincidence this motion, like that in the Senate, was lost by one vote, 20-19. It was obvious that the Senate and the City Council were close to changing their minds about the decision to build civic offices at Wood Quay.

SIGNATURE CAMPAIGN 1978-9

During October and November of 1978, the signature campaign, launched by the Friends of Medieval Dublin after the meeting and the march in September, had been gaining momentum through the country. It was intended to demonstrate to the Government that not merely the citizens of Dublin but the country as a whole wished to preserve the National Monument and were opposed to the proposed high-rise buildings at Wood Quay. The success of the campaign was striking. It was organised on an all-Ireland basis, irrespective of the border, through the co-operation of over eighty societies and associations, including in its wide net bodies such as the Maritime Institute and the Organisation of National Ex-Servicemen. Educational interests were prominent due to the formal support of the various teacher unions. Apart from individuals signing the petition forms, which were addressed to Mr George Colley as the minister responsible, there was public signing of the forms on a succession of Saturdays in public places. The Armagh Historical Society began its impressive list of signatures with that of Archbishop, now Cardinal, Tomás Ó Fiaich.

Pat Russell (right), the Corporation official in charge of the controversial offices project, shows part of Dublin's heritage to Jakob Aano, Rapporteur of the Committee on Cultural Education of the Council of Europe.

The hard evidence for the success of the signature campaign was demonstrated on 23 December when a bearded and befurred Santa Claus (Ian Broad) arrived with a truck at Government Buildings to present Mr Colley with a Christmas present of 70,000 signatures, all neatly arranged in boxes according to counties. These forms were only the first counted section of an accumulation estimated to represent 210,000 signatures.

The inescapable evidence of public feeling came at an awkward time for Mr Pearse Wyse. During the Senate debate of 7 December, he had announced that he hoped to make his 'final recommendation' to the Government the following week. Mr Wyse was deceiving, or was deceived. There were successive statements since September by the Government, by Mr Wyse himself, by the Commissioners of Public Works, indicating that no final decision had yet been taken. In fact, the process of destruction had already been set irrevocably in motion on 29 August when a joint consent explicitly to that effect had been formally signed and sealed between Corporation officials and the Commissioners of Public Works. That was a final decision, but as yet unknown to the public. However, the firm stand taken by the National Monuments Advisory Council, on the need to preserve Wood Quay, caused Mr Wyse to announce, on 14 December, that there would have to be a further meeting with the Council, but when the advice he wanted to hear from it was not forthcoming, no final recommendation was announced. Instead, action was taken by the Corporation, and this precipitated a new crisis.

BACK TO THE COURTS

On 3 January 1979, bulldozers moved into an area of prime archaeological material, at the base of the supporting steel sheeting at Wood Quay, and began to remove material. The thirteen archaeologists working on the site stood literally in front of the bulldozers and forced them to stop. The director of the excavation, Mr Patrick Wallace of the National Museum, was unavoidably absent from the site at the time.

The archaeologists left, and the bulldozers resumed their work of destruction; the archaeologists returned to challenge the machines which stopped once again. It looked as if this cat-and-mouse game would continue indefinitely, with the advantage naturally in favour of the machines. It was in these circumstances that Professor Martin, at the request of the archaeologists, sought for, and secured, a High Court injunction on 10 January, restraining the Corporation from proceeding with the work by bulldozers.

The hearing, which took place before Mr Justice Seán Gannon, attracted widespread notice in the press and will long be remembered by those fortunate enough to attend the court sessions. The plaintiff was Fr Martin with (as in the 1978 injunction) the fiat of the Attorney General, Mr Anthony Hederman. The hearing lasted ten days, involved the taking of oral evidence, the reading of twenty-one affidavits, and legal arguments which were both lively and complicated. The searching examination of statements of Dr Raftery of the National Museum, and of Mr Pascal Scanlon of the Office of Public Works, held the audience spellbound.

One startling fact emerged on the first day of the hearing, namely that formal consent for the demolition of the National Monument had been jointly sealed by the Corporation and the Commissioners of Public Works as far back as 29 August 1978, within two months of the site being declared a National Monument by Mr Justice Liam Hamilton. This all-important fact had not been brought to the notice of the defenders of Wood Quay, nor apparently to the notice of Pearse Wyse, the Government spokesman on Wood Quay. All of his statements on the matter since June 1978 seemed to assume that no final decision had been taken as to the future of the site and he not merely implied but explicitly stated that the final decision rested with the Government. The same assumption, or delusion, underlined the formal debate and motion on the question which took place in the Senate on 6-7 December 1978 and in the City Council on 11 December.

A main argument used by the Corporation in court to justify, on practical grounds, the bulldozing of the archaeological material in this area of the National Monument was the alleged danger of the retaining wall of steel sheeting collapsing on the builder's workers as well as on the archaeologists, and the consequent need to strengthen it with a supporting wall of concrete. The likelihood of any such collapse was queried in an affidavit by Professor Reg Kirwan of Trinity College, an authority on soil conditions as related to engineering. His evidence was strongly supported by another prominent engineering expert, Dr Peter McCabe, who affirmed that the steel sheeting was 'over-structured in every respect; in other words, [was] more than strong enough'.

On 12 February 1979, Mr Justice Gannon delivered judgement, granting, until the hearing of the matter at a full trial, an interlocutory injunction which restrained the Corporation from proceeding with building on the National Monument site. He described the site as of national importance, irreplaceable if destroyed, and beyond value in monetary terms. An even greater issue than Wood Quay emerged when the Judge commented that the concept advocated by senior counsel for the Commissioners of Public Works, 'that administrative officers of the Civil Service are above the law, in relation to their decisions, does not conform to the principles of the Constitution of our democratic State'.

Mr Justice Gannon announced that the issues in question would be dealt with at the trial of the action, which he set for 5 March. That event never came to pass. Within an hour of the High Court decision, the Corporation appealed against it in the Supreme Court, and the hearing took place on 6-7 March before Chief Justice T. O'Higgins and his colleagues, Judges Henchy, Griffin, Kenny and Parke. The judgement of the Supreme Court was unanimous and upheld the appeal of the Corporation and the Commissioners of Public Works against the decision of Mr Justice Gannon. Not only was the injunction discharged but surprisingly the Court dismissed the entire action; the Corporation was free to go ahead with demolition of, and building on, the National Monument; both High Court and Supreme Court costs were awarded against Fr Martin. It was estimated by the media that damages and legal costs would exceed £300,000. A Corporation spokesman stated in the media that Fr Martin would, as a result of the Supreme Court decision, have to meet damages (apart from legal costs) to the tune of £200,000. Five years later, in June 1984, at a hearing in the High Court before Miss Justice Mel Carroll to determine the damages, the Corporation reduced the figure to £89,000 as a personal debt on Fr Martin. But let us return to 7 March 1979 and the Supreme Court decision.

The bulldozers moved in that very evening, as published photographs testify, to rip out as rapidly as possible the invaluable layers of medieval Dublin history. The bulldozed material was carted off in lorries to a Corporation rubbish tip. The evidence was thus totally lost to students of Irish cultural heritage and to the taxpayers who were footing the bill. Corporation bureaucracy, in jackboots, riding high on bulldozers, was in its element.

It was seemingly the end of a legal battle in the Irish Courts, but four days after the judgement of the Supreme Court Fr Martin announced, on 11 March, that, having consulted with his legal advisers, he had decided to take 'the very grave step of applying to the European Commission of Human Rights', claiming that, by virtue of the decision of the Supreme Court, he was the victim of a violation of his rights under both Articles 6 and 13 of the Convention of Human Rights and Fundamental Rights, to which Ireland is a High Contracting Party. The application to the Commission has been lodged at Strasbourg and has not yet been heard, but the necessarily slow legal process did not in any way signify the end of the Wood Quay campaign. In fact many significant decisions and actions followed swift on the heels of the Supreme Court judgement. Before the end of the month some 1,200 people attended a public meeting in the Mansion House, and over 10,000 people again took to the streets demanding preservation of their national heritage. The Wood Quay controversy was far from dead!

RESOLUTIONS AND RUBBISH DUMPS

In late March 1979, the Committee on Culture and Education of the Council of Europe pleaded with the Irish Government to preserve Wood Quay. Two months later, on 11 May, the site was the subject of three resolutions debated and adopted by the Council's Parliamentary Assembly. As well as seeking long-term preservation of the Viking and Anglo-Norman town, the Assembly requested the Irish Government to delay all construction work in the National Monument area and to consult international archaeological opinion. Unfortunately, the Irish Cabinet did not respond, in any positive sense, to the requests of the Council. It is notable that though the Council represents over twenty European countries the only dissenter about Wood Quay at the Parliamentary Assembly was Mr T. Leonard, TD, a Fianna Fáil representative.

Meanwhile, in Dublin, it was apparent that at long last there was a major change of attitude within the City Council. A special meeting of the Council, on 4 May, resulted in a sharp reversal of policy, with the councillors, by a 22-15 vote, requesting a re-negotiation of the contract for the civic offices which would leave the National Monument area free of buildings. During the meeting the Deputy City Manager, Mr Seán Haughey, assured the councillors that building work would only take place on parts of the site archaeologically excavated by scientific methods to bedrock level. Yet, some weeks earlier, on 18 April, Dublin schoolchildren had found a Viking sword on a site where bulldozed material from Wood Quay had been dumped. The sword was described by a spokesman for the National Museum as 'one of the most important such finds ever made'. As the artifact was found out of its archaeological context its contribution to knowledge

Vote For

(Supporters of Save Wood Quay Campaign)

Paddy DUNNE

Hanna BARLOW Community

Robert DOWNES

Mary FLAHERTY

Keep this card

USE YOUR VOTE

Canvass Against

(Names selected on City Council Voting Record, + Statements made on Wood Quay)

Paddy BELTON

Tim KILLEEN

Danny BELL

Billy KEEGAN

TO SAVE WOOD QUAY

Electoral Area No: **3**
Finglas East — Ballymun — Santry — Whitehall etc.

Polling Day ·June 7 1979

Issued by the Save Wood Quay Election Committee

One of eleven electoral area cards published by the Save Wood Quay Election Committee. Those elected in Area 3 were Paddy Dunne, Hanna Barlow, Mary Flaherty and Tim Killeen.

The Sunday World, 10 June 1979.

YESTERDAY'S MAN!

● BATTERED Lord Mayor Paddy Belton muses over his own political obituary in a Dublin pub at lunch-time yesterday. After losing his Dail seat in the last general election, the Lord Mayor Dubliners loved to hate, was drummed out of the Corporation.

The people have spoken.

● FIANNA FAIL COUNT THEIR LOSSES — Page 3

PICTURE: Liam O'Connor.

is obviously slight. What other treasures of art, archaeology, and social history were destroyed will never be known. The importance of full and accurate recording of finds in context was one of the points stressed by many archaeologists at the time. Indeed, the Irish Association of Professional Archaeologists, and the Association of Young Irish Archaeologists, made several public statements highlighting their points of dissatisfaction with the Wood Quay excavations. However, the Corporation officials continued to enjoy the support of a fractional minority of professionals in the field. Writing in *The Irish Times,* on 24 April 1979, Mr Etienne Rynne stated his belief that Dublin Corporation had 'acted most responsibly towards its archaeological obligations'. Later, in the same paper, John Healy dryly expressed the hope that Mr Rynne 'is a better archaeologist than he is a citizen'.

As June approached, concerned citizens took two major and somewhat novel steps – an election campaign and an occupation of the site – to try and give effect to the common wishes of the City Council, as expressed on 4 May, and of the Council of Europe, as expressed on 11 May. The month of June was crucial as the electorate had the opportunity to express their opinion at two levels: local government, and European Parliament. Both elections were scheduled for 7 June.

ELECTION CAMPAIGN AND SITE OCCUPATION

It had been suggested by many people that there should be Wood Quay candidates standing in either or both elections. However, an *ad hoc* group, the Wood Quay Action Group, with the support of the Friends of Medieval Dublin, decided instead to produce 'Vote For, Canvass Against' election leaflets for each of the eleven constituencies represented in the City Council. Over 250,000 leaflets were prepared and distributed. The reaction from the politicians was swift and furious. The general secretary of the Fianna Fáil party accused the *ad hoc* group of trying to intimidate candidates, and stressed that Wood Quay was not a burning election issue. The election results proved him wrong. There was a major change in the personnel of the City Council, and many 'anti-Wood Quay' councillors and candidates were defeated. The most notable of these was the outgoing Lord Mayor, Alderman Paddy Belton, who was a staunch supporter of the civic office complex despite the publicly expressed policy of his own Fine Gael party. Ex-Lord Mayor Belton acknowledged that his defeat was largely due to the stance that he had taken on the National Monument.

The importance of Wood Quay as an election issue was also reflected in the results for the European Parliament, with Michael O'Leary, TD, a professed Wood Quay supporter and one of the prominent citizens who formally occupied the site on 1 June, elected to Europe. Seán Dublin Bay Loftus, who also polled very highly in the Euro-elections, was for many years an outspoken defender of Wood Quay and secured the highest number of votes in the City Council election. Nevertheless, the electorate looked to Dublin City Council for an immediate solution.

The air of optimism on the eve of the first meeting of the new City Council was intense. A clear majority of the new councillors had stated, on election platforms, their determination to save the site. And they meant it. The last few weeks of the

VANDAL OF THE YEAR

BORD FAILTE and the Government are to sponsor a Vandal of the Year competition, it was announced from Dublin Castle last night. The competition is open to Irish people or people of Irish descent in any part of the world. It is hoped to attract vandals from New York, London, Peking, Moscow and Paris for the finals to be held in Dublin at the opening of the Tourist Year. The selection committee would be comprised of members of Dublin Corporation, which has a high international reputation in vandalistic circles. The winner will be presented with a free bulldozer.

The vandals can be male or female and will be judged on abrasive personality as well as good looks and destructive qualities.

The Lord Mayor of Dublin, Alderman Patrick Belton, said that the Vandal of the Year Ball would coincide with the election of the top Irish Vandal. He stressed that only people with proven records in the sphere of vandalism would be allowed to compete. "Clearly, thousands of Irish vandals will want to enter, but we will only accept people whose record as vandals is beyond reproach," he said. The Lord Mayor said that entry would be accepted from some well-known firms whose destructive abilities are legendary.

There will be a contest among the entrants to find out how quickly O'Connell Street can be demolished and turned into a car park.

'O'Brien can shift it'

Wood Quay is to be transferred to Cork as part of a Government Redeployment of Resources Plan, the Taoiseach, Mr Lynch, announced yesterday. In charge of the removal will be the famous Fianna Fail removal man, Willie O'Brien. "I see it as a simple removal job — it will not be in the way in Cork city," he said.

Wood Quay in future, it is understood, will be sited on the River Lee and will be used for the loading and unloading of all Viking ships which come into Cork, according to Friends of Medieval Cork yesterday. They welcomed the transfer of Wood Quay to Cork and said it would be far safer in the southern capital, where there were no vandals to destroy it. "The first thing we will do is to give Wood Quay a thorough cleaning up. We will get rid of all that Viking rubbish, old shoes, jugs and empty Carlsberg bottles," said a Cork preservationist yesterday. "Wood Quay will be made useful in Cork same as the Coal Quay, you know. We don't believe in ornamental stuff that is not useful."

Cork Tourism Ltd. said last night that Wood Quay would be included with Blarney Castle and Glen Rovers Club in the quick American tour of the city. Special "Brian Boru Rules O.K." badges would be distributed from Wood Quay in Cork.

Selling Ireland

"If Wood Quay is successfully transferred to Cork, a number of well-known National monuments will be put on the export market," a spokesman for the Irish Export Market said yesterday. Demolition firms from all parts of the world have been invited to send tenders for the massive demolition jobs which are expected. "This will really get the job-creation scheme off the ground," said Planning Minister Martin O'Donoghue.

Tara, Mellifont, Newgrange, Maynooth, Reginald's Tower, the Giant's Causeway, Arus an Uachtarain, RTE, the GPO, Oisin's Grave, the Rock of Cashel, the Civic Buildings, Croke Park, Blarney Castle and Kilkenny Castle are all under active consideration. Groups of Irish auctioneers have shown prospective German, American, Russian and Chinese buyers over all the National monuments. The usual complaint which they make is that the monuments are lacking in conveniences like lavatories, electric light and

Graffiti on the Wood Quay hoarding.

life of the old City Council saw an increase in the damage being done to archaeological material at Wood Quay. This resulted in an action by a group of prominent citizens to ensure that the site would still be there to be saved by a new Council. On 1 June 1979 the Wood Quay site was occupied.

The occupation, code-named 'Operation Sitric', was not undertaken by delirious academics and long-haired students. Academics and students were among the occupiers, but it was a deliberate occupation by representatives of Irish public life at all levels: from the Dáil, the Senate, the Dublin City Council, major trade unions, by a widow of a former President of the country, and – to show its local grass-roots support – by the chairman of the Liberties Association with supporters from the Oliver Bond flats, as well as by poets, writers, artists and – to give it an Irish flavour – a nun and a priest. The occupation was effected with military precision within a matter of minutes, but was peaceful, and its keynote was effective, gentle, seizure of the site. Militant pacifism.

After twelve nights of occupation, nine people – of the several thousand involved – were served with an injunction obtained by John Paul, the building contractor for the civic office complex. In a High Court hearing before Mr Justice Gannon, on 18 June, the injunction was lifted and jubilation reigned at the site. That same evening the new City Council met and elected Councillor Billy Cumiskey of the Labour Party as Lord Mayor. Mr Cumiskey's first remarks from the chair of the Council, and greeted in the council chamber with thunderous applause, were in the form of an appeal to John Paul to cease construction work until the Council had an opportunity to discuss the entire Wood Quay issue and reach a solution which would entail the preservation of the National Monument. John Paul chose to ignore the request of the Lord Mayor, and instead appealed the High Court decision of 18 June to the Supreme Court. On 21 June the main body of occupiers left the site when the Supreme Court overturned the earlier decision of 18 June.

It was a legal defeat but hopes of a political decision which would save the site were high. These hopes rested on the City Council and, initially, seemed to be justified. Of the 45 elected councillors, 24 signed a motion for debate at a special meeting held on 9 July. The motion, which obviously had a clear majority supporting it, with more than the 24 signatories of the motion, would have effectively stopped all construction work at Wood Quay, and thereby the destruction of Dublin's cultural heritage. Yet, an amazing situation rapidly emerged. Publicly, under extreme pressure, the Lord Mayor dumbfounded everybody, including members of his own party, by ruling the motion out of order A patchwork motion was presented to another special meeting of the Council on 17 July. This motion was passed but was largely ineffective as it merely requested cessation of work pending an estimate for re-design of the complex and clarification as to whether or not the Government would underwrite any such expense.

LOCAL BUREAUCRACY

The members of the Council were obviously willing to try and exercise their political muscle to save the National Monument but they quickly discovered that this muscle was rapidly paralysed. Each attempt to take effective action resulted in a head-on collision with a bureaucratic wall. Legal advices, threats of surcharge, and suggestions of withdrawal of services to councillors were among the barricades raised to prevent the elected representatives giving effect to their election promises. The frustration of the councillors, after numerous debates and special meetings, led them to record formally their feelings as follows in the Minutes of the Council, 19 November 1979:

We, the undersigned members of the Dublin City Council, are opposed to the building of the Civic Office complex, as presently envisaged on the National Monument area of the Wood Quay site, for the following reasons:
1. As public representatives, we feel it is our duty to carry out the democratically expressed wishes of the electorate — as expressed in the local elections, June 1979.
2. The High Court (on 30th June, 1978) declared the area to be a National Monument, i.e., a monument 'the preservation of which is a matter of national importance'. As owners of the area, a major portion of the responsibility for this preservation rests with the Dublin Corporation.
3. The decision of the City Council, in 1977, to go ahead with the building project was based on advices presented to the Council at that time. We now know that these advices were inadequate and/or inaccurate.
4. The concept of totally centralised civic offices is some 25 years old, and now appears to be at variance with present thinking on Local Government reform.
5. We do not accept that the finances already committed to the project would be wasted if the present plans were altered. On the contrary, provision could be made for a scaled-down complex on part of the site, leaving the National Monument portion for development as a cultural and tourist project which would form a key element in the overall approach to medieval Dublin.
6. Dublin Corporation should maintain its concern for inner city renewal (so recently demonstrated in the City Quay area) and ensure suitable development in the Wood Quay area. This does not exclude office development, but does demand that all developments be in sympathy with the historic surroundings.
7. On two occasions this year, May and October, the Parliamentary Assembly of the Council of Europe has issued statements on the Wood Quay situation. The Council specifically noted the role of Dublin Corporation and declared that a re-evaluation of the proposed development would be a gesture warmly welcomed throughout Europe. The Council appealed directly to the Government in May, and in October stated that the Irish Government had not responded. The concern of this European international representative body highlights our responsibility for what is a monument not only of national but also of international importance.
8. The only substantial reasons presented to us for proceeding with building on the National Monument are legal complications which may arise from breaking the contract with John Paul, and financial considerations. We do not accept that these difficulties are

insurmountable and, in fact, we believe they are far outweighed by the reasons presented by national and international experts demanding the preservation of the area.

9. The current excavations at the Fishamble Street portion of the National Monument have resulted in archaeological finds of unique value and interest, including a wooden crozier which is of international significance. It appears that the time being allowed for these excavations (until 21st March, 1980) is quite inadequate and that substantially more time will be needed.

Councillor Mary Robinson
Councillor Michael O'Halloran
Councillor Tony Dunne
Councillor Paddy O'Mahony
Councillor Mary Freehill
Councillor Seán Kenny
Councillor Dan Browne
Councillor Paddy Dunne
Alderman Pat Carroll
Councillor Tony Gregory –
    Community
Councillor William Cumiskey
Councillor Tomás MacGiolla
    (with certain reservations)
Councillor Joe Doyle
Councillor Mrs Alice Glenn
Councillor Mary Byrne
Councillor Declan Ryan

Councillor Mary D. Flaherty
Councillor Michael McShane
Councillor George Birmingham
Alderman Alexis FitzGerald
Alderman Michael Keating, TD
Councillor Michael J. Cosgrave, TD
Councillor Gay Mitchell
Alderman Seán D. Dublin Bay-Rockall
    Loftus *(except I wish a development*
for the Wood Quay site for its tourist
archaeological potential – the Civic
Offices elsewhere)
Alderman Mrs Hannah Barlow –
    Community
Councillor Brendan Lynch –
    Community
Alderman Mrs Carmencita Hederman

Despite this extraordinary step, which the councillors felt necessary to take so that their feelings would be adequately recorded, there was no positive result. No wonder the electorate have come since then to question the whole issue of local democracy in Dublin. Who runs City Hall? The elected representatives of the people, or the entrenched officials?

A STAY OF EXECUTION

The one aspect of the Wood Quay issue, in which the Council was effective, was in terms of acquiring extensions of excavation time. After the occupation ended, excavations on the site re-commenced. A licence, due to expire on 31 March 1980, was issued; the expiry date was later extended to 31 May. On 30 May a statement from the Minister of Finance, Mr Michael O'Kennedy, granted a further two-week extension to allow for 'the final completion' of the excavation. The Council managed to obtain a further three-week extension, which allowed completion, in some fashion, of the area of the site known as Fishamble Street I.

The Government announced, on 10 June, that time and funds would be provided to allow for excavation of the remaining Fishamble Street II area. The time suggested was merely four months but the archaeological team was still on

20 yards of medieval Dublin wall bulldozed

By Maev Kennedy

A TWENTY-YARD stretch of the medieval city wall of Dublin has been bulldozed without any archaeological supervision, because of a continuing row over the terms under which the archaeologists are working.

The wall is being dismantled by agreement between Dublin Corporation and the Office of Public Works, to enable building work to continue. The stones are being numbered and it is intended to re-erect the wall, but grave doubts have been expressed by many archaeologists and historians over the demolition of the oldest city wall in Ireland. The National Museum, as site archaeologists, were invited to stay on and observe the work, but there has been constant disagreement over the facilities offered the archaeologists.

Last Wednesday these disagreements led to the museum's supervisor, Mr Pat Wallace, calling his four workers off the site. It was hoped that this would lead to the work stopping and to negotiations with the builders, but instead the work was speeded up, and a bulldozer was brought onto the site on Thursday night to remove the core material from the wall. Only a small section now remains.

Yesterday morning an *Irish Times* reporter and photographer were both refused admission to the site, and the Corporation's press relations office, in the absence of the chief information officer, refused to give permission to enter.

Last night, Mr Pat Wallace said he was "bitterly disappointed with the whole treatment of the wall."

The unsupervised demolition of the wall has meant the loss of valuable detailed information on the exact techniques used by its builders.

The Keeper of Irish Antiquities in the museum, Mr Michael Ryan, stressed last night that the museum had no responsibility for the wall. "We are not parties to the decision to remove the wall," he said, "and we only agreed to carry out a reporting process subject to certain conditions being met."

Photograph: page 5.

The Irish Times, 1 November 1980.

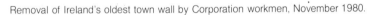

Removal of Ireland's oldest town wall by Corporation workmen, November 1980.

the site as 1981 dawned, and remained there until 21 March. The team was larger than earlier teams, and was still under the direction of the National Museum.

CHANGES IN THE NATIONAL MUSEUM

Just as the Wood Quay saga unfolded under three city managers, Messrs Macken, Molloy and Feely, it also occupied the minds of three directors of the National Museum, Dr Lucas, Dr Raftery and Mr Breandán Ó Ríordáin. Dr Raftery was due to retire from the post in the summer of 1978 but, according to the Department of Education, was retained 'in the public interest', particularly in relation to the Wood Quay saga.

When Dr Raftery did retire, on 11 July 1979, he was replaced by Mr Ó Ríordáin, the former Keeper of Irish Antiquities in the Museum. The appointment was welcomed in many quarters, not least by the Friends of Medieval Dublin, as Mr Ó Ríordáin had been a founding member of the group. Mr Ó Ríordáin's views on Wood Quay were well-known and documented. In the *Taisce* journal, of November-December 1979–January 1980, Mr Ó Ríordáin was quoted as saying that 'This [Fishamble Street] excavation should be carried out in accordance with the highest possible standards — should be done in the best possible way'. Yet some six months later, less than one year after his appointment as Director of the National Museum, Mr Ó Ríordáin effectively condoned the bulldozing of portion of the site. In a letter to Dublin Corporation, on 9 June 1980, he stated:

> I am mindful of the fact that given the constraints placed upon them in the course of their duties the Corporation officials have been most co-operative in matters relating to the archaeological excavation of areas of the Civic Offices site in the past.
>
> Whilst in ideal circumstances we would wish to manually excavate the totality of the site under discussion – to the south of our present excavation – I am of the opinion that – in the event of no other solution being found – the limited area required by the builders to the south of our present excavation site be removed by mechanical means.

The letter was publicly read with considerable satisfaction by a Corporation official at a meeting of the Council on that same day.

The value and importance of Wood Quay, already abundantly clear to national and international experts by 1978, became even more evident with each day of excavation during 1979-81. So, one must look outside the site itself to find the reason for the apparent change of mind shown by Mr Ó Ríordáin. It is not lightly that a Director of the National Museum of Ireland, himself a seasoned archaeologist on medieval Dublin city sites, will condone the destruction of one of the treasures of Ireland, for that is what Wood Quay is, or was, until destroyed.

DEMOLITION OF THE CITY WALL

During October and November 1980 the eleventh-century city wall, which traversed the Wood Quay site, was systematically demolished. The stones of the wall had been ostensibly numbered, prior to demolition, but one must question the assurances given that the wall will be re-built. Throughout the period 1977-1980 the Corporation officials, and their legal representatives, stressed the fact that the wall would be preserved. At one stage, in June 1979, Alderman Ben Briscoe even informed the media that the wall was being preserved at a cost of £10,000 per foot. It is now startling to recall that consent to demolish the National Monument, given jointly by the Corporation and the Commissioners, was subject to the preservation of the city wall. Furthermore, the High Court was told, on 30 November 1977 by Dermot Kinlen, SC for the Corporation, that the wall would be preserved in its entirety; and in a newsletter issued to all Dublin schools, on behalf of the Corporation officials, in November-December 1978, it was stated that the wall 'will be retained exactly where it was originally built'. Yet by November 1980 the wall was almost entirely demolished, portion of it having been bulldozed. Photographs show the machines in action. So much for official promises!

WHERE DOES THE BLAME LIE?

The responsibility for the demolition of the city wall, indeed for the whole cultural *débâcle* at Wood Quay, is shared by many official bodies: the Dublin Corporation (particularly its officials), the Commissioners of Public Works, the National Museum (which, in all fairness it must be noted, did, on at least two occasions, withdraw its personnel who were agonisingly observing the demolition process), and the Government.

The role of the Government was always conveniently clouded. On several occasions, as already noted, Minister of State Pearse Wyse stressed that the ultimate decision was with the Government. Yet, in March 1979, after the Supreme Court decision to uphold the claim of the Dublin Corporation joined with the Commissioners of Public Works to demolish the National Monument at Wood Quay, the Dáil was told by Mr Brian Lenihan (significantly, then Minister for Fisheries) speaking for the Cabinet, that the decision about the fate of Wood Quay ultimately rested with the Dublin Corporation, the legal owners of the site. And 'Dublin Corporation' meant the elected councillors, not the officials, the paid employees. In fact, as we have seen, the councillors were hamstrung by the officials, led by the City Manager, when they wished to halt the building at Wood Quay. However, since the capital expense for the building of the civic offices complex had to come from the Government it was there the real, not the merely legal, decision was taken.

What were the policies of the two successive Prime Ministers, Jack Lynch and Charles Haughey, whose terms of office spanned the years when the finest available Viking-Norman site in western Europe was being systematically destroyed? They probably genuinely regretted what was taking place on the site: the expert butchery by the archaeologists and the rank cannibalism by the bulldozers. They could have intervened, as Jack Lynch did for the Skiddy monument in his native city of Cork, but limited their sympathies to pacifying the archaeologists by a series of subsidies for an accelerated excavation of the site. The immediate bereaved family was thus provided for and effectively silenced, but the vast number of cultural dependents – the Irish nation and western Europe – were deprived of an invaluable inheritance. Jack Lynch stood idly by, but more was expected of Charles Haughey.

Graffiti on the Wood Quay hoarding during the occupation, June 1979.

In December 1979 Charles J. Haughey was elected leader of Fianna Fáil and thereby assumed the office of Taoiseach. His election meant that he had cleverly outmanoeuvered the heir-apparent, George Colley, who as Minister for Finance, had directly condoned the destruction of Wood Quay. It was a rare opportunity for Haughey. His professed awareness and appreciation of the Irish cultural heritage had already been widely publicised by his supporters who projected a beguiling image of the man destined to lead the whole Irish nation to a new level of political and cultural unity. Many felt that he would act swiftly to save the Viking town so recently exposed and so obviously an invaluable part of Ireland's history. An appreciation of the Viking contribution would be a demonstration of a belief in that pluralism without which there cannot be peace and true unity in a re-united country of thirty-two counties. He failed to take the opportunity.

However, by 1982 he showed that he had taken the spirit of the Wood Quay campaign to heart. In that year his government brought two bills before the

Oireachtas, a National Heritage Bill designed to replace the National Monuments Act, and an Urban Development Areas Bill in which medieval Dublin was specifically highlighted as an area where special development controls should be applied. Neither bill got beyond the debate stage because both were shelved with the collapse of the Haughey government. Nonetheless, their introduction to the Dáil and Seanad by Fianna Fáil showed that the defenders of medieval Dublin had finally converted the politicians of all parties to their aims.

Despite this sequel the sad fact remains that the lack of direction from the top political levels in 1979-80 had given the Corporation officials their way and permitted the building of the concrete blockhouses which stand today on the Viking site. There is wry consolation in the fact that every city, including Dublin, should have a permanent monument to ugliness as a grim reminder of what has to be avoided in the future.

Wood Quay money: a drawing by Nick Robinson created during a break in Supreme Court proceedings.

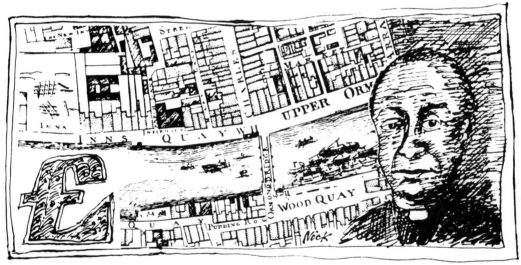

CHAPTER 3

BRIDE ROSNEY

Occupation Diary

Friday 1 June 1979 was the start of the June bank holiday weekend for the majority of Dubliners. For a representative minority it was the day they had chosen for Operation Sitric, an operation described by Fr F. X. Martin as one of militant pacifism.

For years, controversy had raged over the destruction of archaeological material at Wood Quay. Recourse to law had resulted in the declaration that a portion of the site was a national monument, and public pressure ensured that the majority of the city councillors were opposed to what was happening — and they were, at least in theory, the owners of the site and the decision-makers as to its future development. The councillors, at the last meeting of their term of office on 4 May 1979, had instructed the City Manager to negotiate with the building contractors with a view to terminating the contract for the civic office complex and substituting a new contract which would ensure there would be no buildings on the national monument portion of the site and no high-rise buildings on any part of the site. The Council of Europe at its meeting in Strasbourg on 11 May, had also urged that the construction plans be changed and that work on the site be stopped immediately. Yet the destruction continued and in the inevitable vacuum between the effective end of term of the outgoing City Council and the election and first meeting of the new Council there was no one to call a halt. It was in this atmosphere that a group of concerned citizens, who monitored the situation on a daily basis, decided that it was imperative that work on the site cease to ensure that the national monument would not be bulldozed completely before the newly elected members of the City Council had time to implement the decision of their predecessors. As a result, it was reluctantly decided to occupy the site.

Thousands of people had, in the preceding year, indicated their determination to fight in every way possible to preserve Wood Quay. When it became apparent that occupation was the only avenue left, it was felt that the occupying group should be representative of all aspects of Dublin life including cultural, educational, social, political and religious, and that the action should be taken in

Right top: Fr F. X. Martin and Bride Rosney explaining that the occupiers are not prepared to leave.
Right, bottom: Beneath the old town wall poet Thomas Kinsella, accompanied by the signatories, reads the statement to the citizens of Dublin. It ended: 'in order to give time to the incoming city council and to the new City Manager to evaluate the issue and to implement the decision of the last council it is imperative that building work ceases immediately. To allow for this and to meet the desire of the hundreds of thousands who want our heritage saved, for Ireland and for Europe, we have reluctantly taken the decision to occupy the site.'

The Black Raven, symbol of Viking prowess, flies above Wood Quay.

Michael O'Leary surveys the scene outside the barricades.

such a way as to try and avoid confrontation with site personnel or damage to property. The people identified to form the occupying group were:

Kevin Byrne, Alderman of the City of Dublin

Rita Childers, widow of former President of Ireland, Erskine Childers

George Eogan, Professor or Archaeology at University College Dublin

Alexis Fitzgerald, Alderman of the City of Dublin

John Gallagher, Chairman of the Liberties Association

Gemma Hussey, member of the Oireachtas

Oisin Kelly, leading Irish sculptor

Thomas Kinsella, poet and Professor of English at Temple University, Philadelphia

Denis Larkin, trade unionist and former Lord Mayor of Dublin

Mary Lavin, novelist and short story writer

Sr Benvenuta MacCurtain, Dominican nun and lecturer at University College Dublin

Rev F. X. Martin, Professor of Medieval History at University College Dublin and Chairman of the Friends of Medieval Dublin

G. F. Mitchell, former President of the Royal Irish Academy

Michael Mullen, then General Secretary of the Irish Transport and General Workers Union

Donal Nevin, Irish Congress of Trade Unions

Kevin B. Nowlan, Professor of Modern History at University College Dublin

Michael O'Leary, member of the Oireachtas

James Plunkett, author

Michael Scott, architect and founder of ROSC

Imogen Stuart, sculptor

There certainly could not be any accusation that the occupation was carried out by the lunatic fringe — a comment made about the public marches in September 1978 and March 1979.

Ever aware of the efficient grapevine in Dublin, only three people were fully involved in planning the occupation and only one person kept any documentation. Their initial decision was to finalise the date and time for the action. June 1 was selected in the belief that as it was the start of a holiday weekend it should be feasible to occupy the site until the following Monday evening or Tuesday morning at least. The time was selected on the basis that between 7.00 p.m. and 7.15 p.m. each day the construction workers had left the site, the security dogs had not been released and there were only one or two people present on the site, thus the risk of confrontation ought to be slight.

The occupation itself took place in two stages, the site was first entered and secured and then formally occupied. As the 'task force' who were to gain entry were waiting in Winetavern Street the appearance of a Garda squad car increased the pulse rate of many. However the car cruised by with one of the occupants exchanging a friendly wave with Fr Martin. The embarrassed Garda later explained that he assumed, because of the proximity to the Franciscan Church and the presence of a nun and a priest, that he was saluting pilgrims awaiting a bus to Knock. The friendly waves were in fact indicative of the relationship between the Gardai and the occupiers established on that first night and maintained throughout the following three weeks.

The large double gates of the site on Winetavern Street opened just before 7.00 p.m. to allow a car and driver to leave — and the task force to gain entry.

Top: Occupiers tour the site — foreground Michael Scott, Michael O'Leary, Gemma Hussey and Donal Nevin.
Above: At the barricaded front gate, John Gallagher, Paddy Healy, Ald. Kevin Byrne, Bríd ní Craith and Michael O'Brien.
Left: Keeping watch at Winetavern Street Gate, Seamus Kelly, Bride Rosney and Fr F. X. Martin.

Occupiers grouped below the cement mixer which later became the control tower for the site. In the picture left to right are John Gallagher, Oisín Kelly, Alexis Fitzgerald, Bride Rosney, Dennis Larkin, Donal Nevin, Fr F. X. Martin, James Plunkett, (George Eogan behind), Mary Lavin, Michael O'Leary, Sr Benvenuta, Thomas Kinsella, Kevin Byrne and Michael Scott.

They had been alerted that the gates were about to be opened by a flag signal from a house overlooking the area. Immediately they entered, it was made clear to the senior security man present, who was somewhat dismayed to see his former history lecturer at the head of the group, that this was a peaceful protest. The dog kennels on site were secured and the main gate barricaded, allowing access via the pedestrian entrance only. Representatives of the media were alerted as soon as the entry was completed and they were in Winetavern Street in time to meet the formal occupiers arriving; these had grouped earlier in the nearby, and appropriately named, Pious Union Hall! They entered the site at approximately 7.40 p.m. and hoisted a Black Raven flag — the symbolic Viking emblem. They then gathered at the base of the city wall to hear Tom Kinsella read a proclamation to the citizens of Dublin. By this time a large number of Gardai were on duty outside the gate but did not take any action other than to get a list of the occupiers; the site foreman indicated that if the Gardai were not in a position to get Fr Martin and friends out he would contact the bishop.

As word spread throughout the city that an occupation of the Wood Quay site was in progress numerous messages of support arrived. One of the first visitors to the site was welcomed as a modern-day representative of the Vikings; the First Secretary of the Danish Embassy had arrived with seven Danes who lived in Dublin and all pledged their support to the occupiers. Money, food and offers of help continued to arrive throughout the night. The twenty or so people present set to work securing the gates, storing the archaeological artifacts in the Museum huts and preparing sleeping quarters. A roster was drawn up to ensure twenty-four-hour vigilance at the gates, and an emergency procedure, to alert supporters if necessary, was discussed. The two Gardai on duty outside the gates were invited in and joined the occupiers for coffee — they set the scene for their colleagues who generally passed their duty time on site rather than outside. During the night the security man undertook his duties as normal; the guard dogs were not allowed to roam freely as was their custom and good humour prevailed on all sides.

Saturday morning brought dozens of visitors to the site and, unfortunately, the first conflict between the occupiers and the contractors. At approximately 11.30 a.m. an attempt was made to bring a mechanical piledriver in through the south-eastern gate of the site, at the junction of Fishamble Street and Christchurch Place. Once the alert was sounded a group of five occupiers stood in the path of the machine across the entrance to the site. Ten Gardai were present but it was apparent that they were not going to force an entry; one senior officer made it clear that the contractors had a right to go to the courts to have the site cleared of 'unauthorised personnel' and he recommended that the piler be removed and that no attempt be made to proceed onto the site. Eventually, the gateway was secured and the piler moved away. The site foreman, maintenance workers and the security staff were allowed access to the site throughout the day and essential work was facilitated, including the checking of pumps which were used to keep the northern portion free of water.

One of the first visitors of the day was the American Ambassador to Ireland, William Shannon, who was taken on a tour of the archaeological remains as were many others including several members of the Oireachtas and the City Council. A carnival atmosphere prevailed during the afternoon and a press conference was given by Fr Martin and attended by representatives of the majority of the City Council. One of the matters discussed was the need for secrecy in the planning of the occupation. Fr Martin rejected the suggestion that elitist principles had

Construction workers force their way onto the site.

been adopted by the occupying group and explained the need for ongoing security on the site. On Saturday evening a representative group of the occupiers met to review the first twenty-four hours and to establish a routine for the remainder of the time on site. The following rules were proposed and later adopted by a general meeting of all the occupiers:

a   there is one person in overall control of the site at all times. That person will be Fr F. X. Martin or Bride Rosney or a person nominated by them.
There will be two senior duty officers (working on an eight-hour shift basis) assisted by eight junior people. Tasks will be assigned to each person on duty by the two seniors — who will be responsible for the general control of the site while on duty.
b   There will be no alcohol on the site at any time.
c   There will be absolute respect for all property and personnel on the site — including archaeological personnel, contractors and police.
d   No children will be allowed on to the site at any time.
e   Press statements will be issued by those in charge of the site only.

The rules were implemented immediately and everyone settled in for the night. The ten people on duty had the company of two Gardai sitting around the bonfire. All was peaceful until shortly before dawn when the duty officer at the main gate issued a red alert on spotting a number of Gardai, on foot, crossing the Liffey from the direction of the Bridewell. The immediate reaction of fear was compounded when four squad cars and two police vans were noticed coming down from Christchurch Place, i.e. from the direction of Kevin Street. The vehicles pulled in across the road from the site. As everyone was aroused from their sleeping bags to man the gates no one thought of the two Gardai near the fire — who were highly amused at the unfolding chaos. The alert was due to the early-morning Mass at the Franciscan Church which is always frequented by Gardai!

Following this premature rise it was felt that the occupiers were settled in well enough to enjoy a full Irish breakfast. Michael O'Brien tracked down some bacon and sausages and prepared breakfast for all — unwittingly setting the tone for a gourmet day. Lunch saw a choice of beef casserole prepared by Cllr. Pat Carroll's election team or cold turkey prepared by Valerie O'Brien; the fare was such that one Garda telephoned home and pleaded overtime duties. The focal point of the evening meal was trout provided by Barry Desmond TD. The day's menus ensured a continuation of the holiday spirit which was strengthened by the realisation that the guard dogs on site were somewhat less than savage. The only cloud during the day was the discovery that the site toilets had been locked by one of the contractor's staff though in general relations between the two sides remained cordial. Before nightfall the Black Raven flag was supplemented by two sets of streamers sent in by a city florist; the set of black streamers was put on the Four Courts side of the flag while the tricolour flew on the side of the gate controlled by the occupiers.

From the early hours of bank holiday Monday there was an air of tension on the site. Many felt that an injunction might be applied for to ensure that construction work could continue on Tuesday. Cllr. Pat Carroll, Ald. Alexis Fitzgerald, and Donal Nevin of the Irish Congress of Trade Unions addressed a press

Confrontation: Sean Dublin Bay Loftus instructs a construction worker to down tools.

76

EVENING PRESS

Fr F. X. Matin talking to gardai outside the Wood Quay site today.

CONFRONTATION AT WOOD QUAY SITE

conference during the afternoon and focussed attention on trade union reaction to the occupation and the election implications. At a general meeting on the site it was agreed that movements would be monitored from a 'central control tower', a strategically located cement mixer, and announcements would be made as necessary. Plans for the return of construction workers on Tuesday were discussed in detail. It was decided that all items of machinery would be manned with one person sitting in the driver's seat, one person at the front wheels and one at the rear. The Garda authorities were informed of the plans and it was stressed that resistance would be peaceful yet total.

From 6.00 a.m. on Tuesday 5 June, reinforcements to the occupiers began to arrive — the number on site was to be limited to fifty-four and the rest were asked to gather quietly outside. By 8.00 a.m., when the construction workers were gathering in Winetavern Street, all items of machinery were manned. Among the people on site were author Benedict Kiely, actress Sheelagh Richards, Gay Mitchell TD, Ald. Sean Loftus, Cllr. Mary Freehill, Cllr. Pat Carroll, Ald. Carmencita Hederman, author Mary Lavin, poet Seamus Deane, architectural historian Maurice Craig and many of the twenty initial occupiers. Denis Larkin spoke to the site workers as they gathered in Winetavern Street and informed them of their rights as regards pay and employment. Despite his assurances, some thirty workmen forced their way onto the site by breaking through a hoarding on the Christ Church side of the main gate. Various minor scuffles and verbal exchanges took place throughout the morning when the workmen attempted to start up various pieces of machinery and met with passive resistance. The more serious incidents included a high-pressure water hose being turned on a number of protestors, people being hit by fragments of a brick thrown into a concrete mixer, an attempt to move a dumper truck in which author James Plunkett was sitting and the operation of pneumatic drills. During the morning it became apparent that the security man on site was concerned about insurance cover in the event of an injury and there was no further attempt to start work. By lunch hour the following notice had been posted in several locations throughout the site:

No liability whatsoever will be accepted for injury to persons or damage to property while on this site without the express permission of John Paul Construction Ltd.

T. Lloyd
Contracts Manager.

Good humour was restored by the visit to the site of RTE personality Mike Murphy, who had consistently been a supporter of Wood Quay, and by mid-afternoon construction workers were posing for photographs with Fr Martin.

By nightfall plans for a continuation of the passive resistance shown during the day had been finalised and an air of confidence was apparent. There was a general feeling of having won the first battle but an awareness that the war was yet to come.

Wednesday morning was dull and overcast and as the protestors manned the machines it began to drizzle. Shortly before 9.00 a.m. some twenty workmen broke part of the fence and entered the site, and, as reported in the newspaper, 'a middle-aged helmeted man, who appeared to be a senior official on the site,

Above: Construction workers pour water through the hole which they made in the 'bunker' (canteen) roof.

Left: Biddy Reid, victim of an attack.

raised the temperature'. Indeed he did! There was an attempt to pull one occupier from her perch on a fence; a large barrel was pushed over narrowly missing Mary Lavin; bicycles belonging to the occupiers were kicked and thrown about and the contents of a cup were thrown at two people on gate duty. An assault on the flags and banners over the main gate followed – the jib of a crane was swung out over Winetavern Street several times and succeeded in tearing the Old Dublin Society and the Liberties Association banners; however the symbolically important Black Raven was saved due to the prompt action of a journalist. Indeed several journalists joined protestors in standing inside the tent to ensure that it would not be the next object of the crane's attention. Meanwhile, the people sitting on the compressor, located directly under the cliff face at John's Lane (an area known as Sitric's Well), were drenched by water poured from the top of the cliff. The light drizzle of the early morning had turned into a heavy downpour shortly before noon when seven of the workers got on the roof of the concrete 'bunker' just inside the main gate and freed a blocked drain with a pickaxe. This resulted in a deluge of water into the bunker, right on top of the storage area and food table of the occupiers. After a lunchtime respite, hostilities resumed at about 3.00 p.m. when a high-pressure hose was turned on one of the occupiers — an action which resulted in a report of assault to the Gardai. Tensions were very high and both sides feared more serious incidents would occur on the following day. As a result, a meeting was arranged between representatives of the protestors and the site foreman with a view to reaching a peace treaty. The following points were agreed to:

a A maximum of thirty-two workers would be allowed in through the gate each day. They would come in singly and not try to rush the gate.
b The gate would be controlled by the occupiers.
c The pumps were the only items of machinery to be touched.
d The workers would be engaged in rock scraping and breaking in Sitric's Well.
e The toilets would be reopened.

The details of the treaty were accepted by the occupiers at a general meeting that night and, with the exception of those on duty, everyone retired feeling confident that the following day would see no confrontation on the site and a successful day at the ballot box.

Thursday 7 and Friday 8 saw everyone on the site preoccupied with elections and with the production of the first issue of the *Wood Quay Occupation News*. Initially, there was concern that the time and money invested in the election campaign might not be a dramatic success. A massive canvas had been undertaken in each electoral area of the city and cards were distributed asking for support for the pro-preservation candidates and a rejection of others. It was a novel idea and certainly worried many politicians who found themselves being actively canvassed against. The distribution of some 200,000 cards ensured that Wood Quay was a major election issue — and the work was certainly justified. Elation was high as word came through from the counts that supporters like Mary Robinson, Pat Carroll, Sean Loftus, Carmencita Hederman, Mary Freehill and Alexis Fitzgerald were doing well in the polls; but the sweetest moment was undoubtedly when confirmation came that the outgoing Lord Mayor, Paddy

Fr F. X. Martin escorts Senator Mary Robinson onto the site, while John Gallagher stands above on guard duty.

The creative adaptation of an advertisement by the construction workers.

Right: The second issue of *Wood Quay Occupation News.*

Belton, had lost his seat. During the previous year Mr Belton had been a most outspoken opponent of the preservation lobby and had differed with his own party on the issue. He later acknowledged the effect his stance on Wood Quay had on his election chances; indeed his place on the City Council was taken by Mary Flaherty who declared, 'It was Wood Quay which defeated Mr Belton'.

The *Occupation News,* edited by Michael O'Brien, was published on Friday night and went on general sale on Saturday. The paper featured articles on the background to the occupation and the events of the first few days. The confidence of the people involved was indicated by the fact that it was billed as issue number 1 and copyright was held by St Olaf's Press of Wood Quay.

By Saturday 9 the only election results outstanding were those from the European elections and three of the candidates involved, Sean Loftus, Michael O'Leary and John O'Connell, spent much of the morning on the site. The Council of the Academy of Letters held their meeting on the site as a gesture of support and a welcome evening visitor was Dr Garret FitzGerald, leader of the opposition, who pledged his personal support and that of the Fine Gael group on the City Council. However, the day was not all bright as water was rising on the northern

·OUR ELECTION VICTORY.

The news that Lord Mayor Paddy Belton had been sacked by the people of his Dublin constituency was unreservedly welcomed behind the barricades here at the Wood Quay site. No-one in Irish public life has opposed preservation more strenuously than Mr. Belton. There can be little doubt that those who suffered his frequent outbursts in the chamber at City Hall must feel that Irish political life could only be enriched by the passing of Belton into oblivion.

Only once in every five years do the people have an opportunity to intervene

portion of the site and an engineer's investigation indicated that parts had been removed from all three pumps rendering them inoperable. No occupiers had been near the pumps but they had been regularly checked and 'maintained' by the contractor's staff. The Secretary of John Paul Ltd. was sent a copy of the engineer's report together with a covering letter explaining the occupiers concern that if the rising water level were to reach the foot of the old city wall it might easily lead to erosion of the clay foundations and a subsequent collapse. By Monday morning the pumps were restarted and the water level was receding which left the Viking 'ship', which had been launched on the temporary Sitric's Lake, high and dry.

At a meeting between representatives of the two sides on Monday afternoon it was agreed that items of machinery could be moved one at a time to facilitate servicing but that once moved they would not be returned to their original positions. This resulted in a happier workforce as they felt they were engaged in more productive work than when scraping rock in Sitric's Well; the job of the occupiers was also easier as the machines were gradually being moved to one small area of the site.

Issue number 2 of the *Wood Quay Occupation News* was published on Tuesday 12, complete with a short story by James Plunkett, which, not surprisingly, was entitled 'Sitting in a Dumper', and a specially written poem by Tom Kinsella. The paper highlighted the defeat of Paddy Belton and the arrival of three kittens in the Casey home at Fishamble Street, the kittens were to be called F, X and Martin! One of the celebrity visitors during the day was Peter O'Toole who was in Dublin for the filming of *Strumpet City*. Like others who were taken on a tour of the site, he expressed disbelief that the Civic Office project had been proceeded with for so long. A peaceful day on the site — the calm before the storm.

On the morning of Wednesday 13 June, John Paul & Co. Ltd. were granted a temporary injunction restraining nine named defendants from trespassing on the

Halt demolition of Wood Quay: Dr. FitzGerald

DEMOLITION work being done on the Wood Quay site could cause irretrievable damage, claimed **Dr. Garret FitzGerald**, leader of Fine Gael, yesterday in the Dail. He said the Government had a responsibility in the matter.

The Ceann-Chomhairle, **Mr. Joseph Brennan**, said Dr. FitzGerald had earlier raised the matter with him but he had not been able to establish in the time at his disposal what Government accountability might or might not be in the matter.

He could not, therefore, agree to have the matter raised in this way at this time. There were other procedures which the deputy might try. The deputy could raise the matter again next Tuesday.

Dr. FitzGerald urged that a decision be given later in the day.

Otherwise the whole procedure whereby urgent matters could be debated at once would be defeated. The procedure was there to allow things to be stopped.

The **Ceann Chomhairle** said the matter could not be raised later in the day.

The Labour Party leader, **Mr. Frank Cluskey**, said as the Taoiseach was present surely he could indicate whether or not they had responsibility in the matter.

Dr. FitzGerald recalled that a statement had been made last December in the Seanad by the

Mr. Jack Lynch

Dr. Garret FitzGerald

the site had already started and all their talk would be redundant within a few days. "If this matter is not raised today there will be no matter to discuss next Tuesday."

Mr. Cluskey asked if the

regard to Wood Quay in the light of the Supreme Court decision which cleared the way for Dublin Corporation to build civic offices on the site.

The Minister for Fisheries, **Mr. Lenihan** said the Government

is likely to equal those discovered in the areas recently excavated, around 1,500, and that the area is crucial. How could the Minister reconcile the previous statements and avoid the conclusion that the Minister of State misled the public and the Senate, asked Dr. FitzGerald.

Will the Minister not accept that at 6.15 p.m. yesterday bulldozers moved in to tear down and destroy many layers of civilisation?

Mr. Lenihan replied he was not saying that the Government had no function in the matter. It was not he (the Minister, standing in for the Taoiseach) who was saying it — it was the Supreme Court. Basically, what the Court had found was that the Government did not have any function in the matter and that it was purely a matter of

Looking in at Wood Quay

Fine Gael leader, **Dr. Garret FitzGerald**, is shown around the Wood Quay site in Dublin by Bride Rosney, **secretary of the occupation group, during his visit to the site last evening.**

Dr Garret FitzGerald, then leader of the Opposition, raised the issue in Dáil Éireann (*Irish Independent*, 9 March 1979) and lent his support while visiting the site.

Wood Quay site. The nine defendants were: Fr F. X. Martin, Bride Rosney, Seamus Kelly, Leo Swan, Pat Healy, Seamus O'Reilly, Richard Haworth, Michael O'Brien and John Gallagher. News of the injunctions was initially relayed by members of the press and later confirmed when seven of the nine defendants were served with copies of the court order. Two of the defendants were not on the site and did not receive a copy until the following day. On the Wednesday afternoon the seven 'injunctees' on site held a meeting, and the poet Peter Fallon and politician Gemma Hussey stood guard at the door of the tent. There seemed to be some dismay amongst the contractor's staff when, following the meeting, the seven looked for tea rather than help to pack their bags. Many of the following forty-eight hours were taken up with various legal discussions. There were two teams of barristers and solicitors involved, and one of the defendants was representing himself.

The court hearing was scheduled for the following Monday morning and it was quite evident that there was no shortage of volunteers to keep the site fully manned until that time. In the interim there was intense political activity and affidavits for the hearing were sworn by Cllr. Pat Carroll, representing Labour, and Ald. Alexis Fitzgerald, representing Fine Gael. They stated their belief that it was the wish of the newly elected Council to save the archaeological remains at Wood Quay and that immediate steps would be taken to halt construction work. The numbers of visitors to the site swelled enormously over the weekend and there was much angry reaction to an article in the *Sunday World* entitled 'Screw Wood Quay — it's costing you a fortune'; this was the first adverse editorial comment from a national newspaper — and the only one.

Monday 18 June was perhaps the most eventful day since the beginning of the occupation. The injunction hearing was listed for the morning in front of Mr Justice Gannon but did not in fact commence until approximately 2.30 p.m. By 3.20 p.m. it was all over, the injunction having been lifted and the Judge having indicated that it was not the appropriate remedy for the contractors to have sought. By 4.00 p.m. there was a joyful reunion on the site with the nine 'injunctees' and dozens of supporters. The new City Council met for the first time that evening with the sole item being the election of the Lord Mayor. In his acceptance speech following his election, Cllr. Billy Cumiskey asked that all work on the Wood Quay site should cease until a section 4 motion (obliging the City Manager to obey) had been tabled on 25 June. It was agreed that the councillors would be given an opportunity to tour the site before the following meeting. At the Lord Mayor's reception in the Mansion House after the meeting it was announced that the first official visit of the Lord Mayor on the following morning would be to the occupied site. Little wonder that the occupiers retired elated and full of confidence — every battle to date had been won.

True to his word, Cllr. Cumiskey arrived on the site at about midday on Tuesday and spent a lot of time talking to occupiers and to site workers. He then went on a full tour of the archaeological remains. Shortly after his departure a journalist arrived on site to get reaction from the 'injunctees' to the appeal lodged with the Supreme Court against Mr Justice Gannon's judgement of the previous Monday. The reaction was to find out all that the journalist knew as the defendants had heard nothing. There were lengthy discussions that night and the following morning and, although there was obvious concern about the appeal, there was total confidence that the task initiated was almost completed. The occupiers had held the site long enough for a new City Council to take office and the ball was now firmly in their court. As a result, and following legal advice, eight of the nine defendants issued a statement on Wednesday night. It stated:

When we reluctantly took the decision to occupy the Wood Quay site on 1 June, we said we were doing so to maintain the integrity of the National Monument until such time as a new City Council had been elected and had had an opportunity to assume their political responsibility for the site. This has now happened and the Council are holding a special meeting on next Monday to discuss the entire, complex issue. We view this as a vindication of our action and expect that the overwhelming majority of the City Council, who have committed themselves to the preservation of the National Monument, will vote in favour of a motion to cease construction activity. We also expect the establishment of a committee to discuss the form and scale of buildings suitable for the remainder of the site.
We have been particularly heartened by the visit to the site of the newly elected Lord Mayor of Dublin – on his first day in office – and by the

Fr F. X. Martin addressing the occupiers, with Bride Rosney and Donal Nevin on the right.

Occupiers discussing tactics: from left to right, Gary O'Callaghan, Richard Haworth, Leo Swan, Simon Devilly, Michael O'Brien, Bride Rosney, Fr F. X. Martin.

concern he has displayed for a speedy settlement of the situation. This action, following on the Lord Mayor's request that building work should cease pending a Council decision, has helped us to decide that we should vacate the site immediately. We have done so this afternoon in the expectation that the correct decision for the future of Wood Quay will be reached after the issue has been thrashed out at a political level.

The occupation continued, however, and was still in force on Thursday 21 when the Supreme Court sat at 11.00 a.m. The court rose at 11.50 a.m. to allow the defendants' counsel to get information as to the presence of trespassers on the site. Following a hurried visit by legal representatives, all but two of the occupiers accepted advice to leave. The court re-sat at 12.00 noon and rose for lunch shortly afterwards. Judgement was delivered at 2.00 p.m. and the court granted the injunction to John Paul & Co. Ltd. and warned that the occupiers seemed to have incurred criminal responsibility as well as making themselves liable for damages on a massive scale. By the time the defendants left the court, rockbreakers were at work on the site despite the Lord Mayor's request.

However the day and the effective end of the occupation ended, almost literally, on a high note with the recording of Cormac O'Duffy's song 'You can't take away Wood Quay' at the Keystone Studios. Meanwhile the editor of the *Wood Quay Occupation News* was finalising issue number 3, including a report of the day's events under the heading 'Twenty Glorious Days'.

Top: Immobilised digger; Gary O'Callaghan (standing) looking at Phil Moore (in the cab) and Heather King (in the bucket).

Above: A cartoon from the *Wood Quay Occupation News*.

Right: Rita Childers, Mary Lavin, Rachel Hussey, Anne-Charlotte Pedersen and Gemma Hussey.

Some of the people who occupied or visited the site (from the visitors book)

Éamonn Mac Thomáis, author
Mary Lavin, short story writer
Thomas Kinsella, poet
Peter Fallon, poet and publisher
James Plunkett, author
Oisin Kelly, sculptor
Maurice Craig, author and architectural
  historian
Agnes Bernelle, actress
Imogen Stuart, sculptor
Sheelah Richards, actress
Eamon Morrisey, actor
Ben Kiely, writer
Val Mulkerns, writer
Seamus Deane, poet
Bob Carlile, Abbey actor
Mike Murphy, RTE presenter
Gene Martin, RTE producer
Liam C. Martin, artist
Hilary Boyle, writer
Eavan Boland, poet
Patrick Boyle, writer
Mervyn Wall, writer and former Arts
  Council Chairman
Ulick O'Connor, writer
Peter O'Toole, actor
Elizabeth Shannon, writer and wife of USA
  ambassador

William Shannon, then USA ambassador
  to Ireland
Donal Nevin, trade unionist
Denis Larkin, trade unionist
Nicholas Maxwell, archaeologist, former
  assistant director of Wood Quay
  excavations
Claire Foley, archaeologist of Historic
  Monuments Branch, Belfast
George Morrison, writer and film producer
Paddy Shaffrey, town planner
Maura Shaffrey, architect
Michael Scott, architect and founder of ROSC
Eithne de Valera, grand-daughter of
  former president
Emer de Valera, Bean Uí Chuiv, daughter
  of former president
Brian O Cuiv, senior professor,
  Institute of Advanced Studies
Muriel McCarthy, Marsh's Library and Old
  Dublin Society
Charles Gray-Stack, Dean of Ardfert
Thomas Salmon, Dean of Christ Church
  Cathedral
Erwan Touere, Environmental
  Commission, EEC
Earl Layman, Historic Preservation Officer
  for the City of Seattle, USA
Patrick Henchy, Chester Beatty Library

Nick Robinson, the Heritage Trust

Jerry Sheehan, Director of Consumer Affairs, EEC

Tim Creedon, member of the National Monuments Advisory Committee of the Board of Works

Rita Childers, widow of former president

Phil Moore, Women's Political Association

William Cumiskey, Lord Mayor and Labour councillor on Dublin Corporation

Mary Robinson, Labour councillor on Dublin Corporation, member of the Oireachtas

Mary Flaherty, Fine Gael councillor on Dublin Corporation, member of the Oireachtas

Joe Doyle, Fine Gael councillor on Dublin Corporation, member of the Oireachtas

George Bermingham, Fine Gael councillor on Dublin Corporation, member of the Oireachtas

Pat Carroll, Labour alderman on Dublin Corporation

Alexis Fitzgerald, Fine Gael alderman on Dublin Corporation, member of the Oireachtas

Kevin Byrne, Community alderman on Dublin Corporation

Carmencita Hederman, Community alderman on Dublin Corporation

Hannah Barlow, Community alderman on Dublin Corporation

Sean Loftus, Community alderman on Dublin Corporation, former member of the Oireachtas

Eric Doyle, Fine Gael councillor on Dun Laoghaire Borough Council

Jane Dillon Byrne, Labour councillor on Dun Laoghaire Borough Council

Gay Mitchell, Fine Gael councillor on Dublin Corporation, member of the Oireachtas

John O'Connell, former MEP, member of the Oireachtas

Michael O'Leary, former MEP, member of the Oireachtas

Barry Desmond, member of the Oireachtas, now government minister

Gemma Hussey, member of the Oireachtas, now government minister

Garret FitzGerald, member of the Oireachtas, now Taoiseach

Una O'Higgins O'Malley, local election candidate

Prof. K. B. Nowlan, UCD

Prof. George Eogan, UCD

Sr. Benvenuta MacCurtain, UCD

Prof. Conor Martin, UCD

Prof. Paddy Meehan, UCD

Hilary Jenkins, UCD

Terry Barry, TCD

L. M. Cullen, TCD

Wm. J. Davis, TCD

Prof. Gus Martin, UCD, former member of the Oireachtas

Trevor West, TCD, member of the Oireachtas

Fr Martin Nolan, General of the Augustinian Order

There were many others ...

A meeting of the Irish Academy of Letters was held on the site during the occupation. From left: Thomas Kinsella, Patrick Boyle, Mary Lavin, James Plunkett, Eavan Boland and Mervyn Wall.

Lord Mayor Billy Cummiskey signing the visitors book, with Richard Haworth and Fr F. X. Martin (right) and Rachel Hussey (left).

Jean Norton on gate duty, observing a chat between a garda and occupiers.

The daily press conference (looking across the site towards Fishamble Street). On the platform are Gemma Hussey, Fr F. X. Martin, Tom MacWilliams (site foreman), Richard Haworth and Bride Rosney. The tent in which some of the occupiers slept is in the centre of the picture and the abandoned building works are in the background.

No. 3   June 1979   Price 25p

WOOD QUAY NEWS

IT'S OVER TO YOU, JACK

In the long run the funds to re-locate the office and develop the Wood Quay site properly come from central government.

The electorate have given their verdict, now it's up to the government to respond. Wake up Jack and George, let's have this long awaited decision.

Black Raven, symbol of Odin, hovering over Wood Quay.

THE HIGH COURT

As a result of a temporary injunction which was granted by Mr. Justice Hamilton on the 13th June, the "Wood Quay 9", i.e. the nine members of the occupying group who were named in the document, appeared at the High Court on Monday the 18th June. The atmosphere in the packed courtroom was tense as Mr. Justice Gannon opened the proceedings. Sworn statements from both parties were presented and Mr. Francis P. Murphy S.C. (for the construction company) began by outlining the reason why he proposed that an injunction should be granted. Other affidavits were sworn by F. X. Martin and two others of the '9'. were read. Significantly, an affidavit of the representatives of the Fine Gael and Labour groups, namely Councillors Alexis FitzGerald and Dan Browne outlined their belief that a City Council motion preventing further destruction of the National Monument was imminent and that it would have majority support on the new City Council. Fr. Martin pointed out in his affidavit that the City Council

20 GLORIOUS DAYS

"Peace! We come in peaceful protest" said F. X. Martin, O.S.A., to the astonished doorman as he entered Wood Quay on Friday June 1. The protest was against the laying of concrete and the digging of foundations for tower blocks at a time when the Corporation Council had asked the City Manager to enter into negotiations with the contractor. It was a protest for the rights of democracy against the inertia of bureaucracy, for the wishes of the citizens of Dublin against the wishes of the Corporation. These wishes were clearly shown by the voters during the protest. Paddy Belton, Ray Fay, Lauri Corcoran and Sean Kelly are gone. A new Council, pro- Wood Quay has been elected. Three weeks of no destruction, and time for the Council to consider its views were gained by the protest.

The personal request made by the new Lord Mayor William Cumiskey to John Paul & Co. to stop building work on the National Monument together with his visit to the site and that of the City Councillors and Aldermen shows the willingness of the Council to not only agree with but take on the responsibilities and sentiments of the protestors.

This twenty-day protest both in its personalities, execution and success was unprecedented. Although the Supreme Court has found against the protestors, Wood Quay will be saved.

meeting of May 4th had already requested that the City Manager renegotiate the contract in order to preserve the national monument site at Wood Quay.

Mr. Justice Gannon having considered the elements of the case delivered his verdict. He identified two main aspects of the case (a) the trespass for which he deemed a High Court Injunction inappropriate; (b) the contract between the Corporation and the construction company. He argued that it was a pity that the parties should seek to use the courts as an instrument for 'jousting'. He referred to the matter of trespass and he deemed that this was not a sufficient reason for continuing the injunction.

Messengers were sent to the site as soon as the verdict was known and a notice was put outside the front gate which read 'Injunction removed, justice has been done'..

When F. X. Martin arrived he received a hero's welcome and was greeted at the site by clapping, cheering and an impromptu rendering of the Wood Quay ballad. He immediately declared that the occupation was still on.

1.

A TREASURED
PAST

CHAPTER 4

PETER WALSH

Leaves from a Retrospective Photo Album

The Wood Quay site is but one of the areas in the old walled city which are rich in archaeological material and where the architecture of the streetscapes has vanished. A curtain of silence has been drawn over popular and academic literature on the topography of old Dublin, particularly for the period c.1860-1960. Indeed, illustrative material of the changing vistas of the old city has not been put to serious use since the publication of Strangways and McDowell Cosgrave's *Illustrated Dictionary of Dublin* in 1895. Photographs, unfortunately, have become such a commonplace in our time that their historical value has been ignored until fairly recently. To some extent, the Victorians may be excused. Photographs taken on the spot were often copied by artists for easily-reproduced engravings before the use of the half-tone process became common. Artistic licence and unwitting errors frequently debased the authenticity of such views, though engravings are valuable nonetheless in that they often reveal information not recorded elsewhere.

A living city is constantly changing. For Dublin this process was slowed down in the first half of the seventeenth century due to civil strife. The medieval character of its streets was compared with that of Bristol's by Luke Gernon in 1620 when he called it a 'city of timber'; it was not until after 1640 that brick nogging was introduced to the city's cagework buildings. The charming blend of brick and stone so typical of the Georgian city only emerged during the alterations of the seventeenth, eighteenth, and early -nineteenth centuries. For close on three hundred years, come dawn and dusk, the city was tinged with the pigeons'-breast shading immortalised in the watercolours and aquatints of Malton.

For Wood Quay, as for other sites within the city, the photograph is of inestimable value in reconstructing the former appearance of the area, and there follows here a 'baker's dozen' of views no longer to be enjoyed. They highlight the ongoing destruction of those often little-known wonders which have made Dublin so unique in the past. Some are far from perfect and for these no apology is made; they are printed for their historical interest. Attributions are given where known, although one or two remain anonymous.

Plate 1. This shows Christ Church Cathedral from the south-east as it appeared in the autumn of 1870. Part of the fourteenth-century long choir constructed for

Plate 1. Photograph by Millard and Robinson. Courtesy Guinness Hop Store collection.

John de St Paul is shown on the right. A small fragment of this choir is still preserved in the cathedral grounds. The clock in the tower, which replaced an older one in 1845, had a once famous feature: a pendulum eighteen feet long.

Plate 2. Just as the north aspect of Christ Church was revealed by demolition work in the late 1960s, the now familiar view of the east end of the cathedral was exposed for the first time when Lord Edward Street was laid out in the 1880s. The official opening ceremony was performed in July 1886 by the Rt Hon T. D. Sullivan, sometime Fenian, Land Leaguer, Parnellite MP, and at that time Lord Mayor of Dublin.

The Inchicore Horse-tram with the back-to-back knifeboard seats on its open top, empty now and nearing the end of the run, is passing the bricked-up pedimented rere entrance to Tom McNally's. Since the 1860s the McNally Brothers, provision merchants and lard and tallow refiners, operated from numbers 13, 14 and 15 Copper Alley – the medieval Preston's Lane – and part of their extensive premises can be seen on the extreme right. The pony and cart

Plate 2. Photographer unknown. Courtesy Thomas Hayden.

behind the tram are alongside the junction with Pembroke Court which, from the seventeenth century, connected Copper Alley with Castle Street. The couple walking by the wall beyond the cart are treading the line of Saul's Court which, like Copper Alley, intersected Fishamble Street. It was named after Laurence Saul, an eighteenth-century Roman Catholic distiller who was prosecuted in 1759 for harbouring a co-religionist; he fled the country and died in France in 1768. In 1868 there remained four tenements 'at Saul's Court off No. 8 Fishamble Street' rateably valued from £4 to £9.

Plate 3. The east end of Christ Church as seen in 1895, showing the then new library built as an extension to the Chapter House.

Until the mid-1890s Fishamble Street officially extended from Castle Street to Essex Quay. In preparing the ground for the western entrance to Lord Edward Street in the early 1880s numbers 5 to 10 Fishamble Street were demolished. Numbers 5 and 6 were in effect a rere entrance to James Green & Co., tea, wine and spirit merchants, who operated out of number 35 Castle Street. A decade earlier, in 1870, William Day, basket maker, was at number 7 and John J. Roe, clothes dealer, was at number 8, on the corner of Saul's Court. The individuals then lodging at numbers 9 and 10 were Charles Lennox, 'piece broker', and Edward Foresman, tailor.

Not far from here the unhappy James Clarence Mangan was born on May Day 1803. A most prolific poetic genius and the son of an unsuccessful publican, he began work as a copying clerk in a scrivener's office at the age of fifteen, and remained one for ten years. He struggled for a living by contributing articles and poems to literary publications and he worked for a short time in Trinity College

Plate 3. Photographer: E. MacDowell Cosgrave. Source: *The Illustrated Dictionary of Dublin,* 1895.

Library. Something approaching fleeting happiness was afforded him during his short time with the Ordnance Survey Office, where, although employed in a very minor capacity, he enjoyed the company of O'Donovan, Petrie and O'Curry. Always a melancholic young man, aggravated by years of badly-paid drudgery and an ill-fated love affair, he became addicted to opium and alcohol and spent his last years in wretchedness and neglect, dying at the age of forty-eight in the Meath Hospital.

To the right of the cathedral can be seen the entrance to John's Lane East, the southern boundary of the Wood Quay site. Numbers 1 to 3 are shown, then set in tenements.

Plate 4. Photographer: P. Healy.

Plate 4. St John's Lane East takes its names from the church dedicated to the Evangelist which formerly stood at its eastern end. This view, looking west on a December day in 1966, shows the houses once occupied by the Vicars Choral of Christ Church, part of the northern face of which can be seen on the left. Under the Synodal Act of 1872 two unpaid 'residentiary canons' were appointed and given the duty of conducting the choral services in the cathedral. By this date however, the choristers had long given way to other tenants. Of the eleven houses in the lane during the early 1870s, three were occupied by tailors, one other by a carpenter and, apart from Mrs Murphy's remnant shop at number 6, the remainder were set in tenements. A century earlier another tailor from John's Lane named Flood, who was a noted tennis player, changed his needle and thread for the mask and turned highwayman.

A Royal or Real Tennis Court was to be found off this lane from the time of James I. The entrance to this court was through number 4 John's Lane and can be seen clearly in the photograph. This racquet court retained its spectators' gallery and marker's box until 1810. The end wall of the court remained until May 1978, when it was demolished.

Throughout the medieval period the ground on which these houses were built was held on lease from the Dean and Chapter by taverners and vintners whose cellars are often described as having been located under Christ Church. In the early seventeenth century perhaps the most highly coloured name applied to one of these wine cellars was 'Hell'. It appears that the effigy of the devil from this old house in John's Lane was removed to a passage on the south side of the cathedral about the year 1680. This by-way, immortalised by Robbie Burns, the poet friend of adopted Dubliner Alexander Findlater, adjoined the Old Law Courts and sported a wooden figure of 'Old Nick'.

During the sixteenth and seventeenth centuries the overspill of butchers and fishmongers from Fishamble Street erected stalls against the wall of St John's Church here. These were finally condemned as 'noisesome' by the Court of King's Bench in 1682 and were pulled down. A parochial order was made that no stalls or shops would ever again be erected against the church. At this time St John's was rebuilt but apparently neither sure, safe, nor soundly, as it was again to be reconstructed eighty years later.

It was here in 1842 that Dr Madden found Anne Devlin and brought her to Butterfield Lane. This frail tragic figure, widow of the labourer Campbell, who forty years earlier protected the rash young Emmet and who, from her solitary cell in Kilmainham, spurned Major Sirr's offers of cash and comfort, was to die in the most abject poverty in a room in Little Elbow Lane off the Coombe in 1851.

Plate 5. A glimpse here of some of the buildings which stood on the Fishamble Street perimeter of Wood Quay. The curve of the street leads the eye into the heart of the parish of St Olaf. In the middle distance is the last surviving occupied residence in this ancient street. It stands on the north-west corner of what was known until 1840 as Smock Alley, now Essex Street, West, beyond which St. Tullock's Lane ran down to the Fish Slip. Auditor-General Sir James Ware, father of the antiquary of the same name, died suddenly as he was walking through Fishamble Street to his home in Castle Street in 1632.

On the corner of Lord Edward Street is the Working Boys' Home and Harding Technical School. The home was founded in 1877. In 1886 the money bequeathed by Miss Harding was given on condition that a technical and night school should be opened in connection with the home. With part of this money the present building was erected in 1892. It has a frontage of 162 feet to Lord Edward Street, and is built after an Elizabethan style of red brick with buff

Plate 5. Photographer: E. MacDowell Cosgrave. Courtesy R.S.A.I.

terracotta facings from the design of Albert Murray. It had a large lecture hall, two school rooms, a dining hall and dormitories for sixty boys. There are four shops on the ground floor.

Down Fishamble Street can be seen the wall of the Corporation Yard which, when the photograph was taken in 1893, straddled the former entrance to Molesworth Court where, from the press of John Harding, Swift's 'Drapier's Letters' were issued in 1724. The four-storey building beside the yard – number 48 and 49 under the old numbering and occupied by Matthew Moran, general carrier – was the site of the old Fleece Tavern and the entrance to Fleece Alley was through this building. This narrow passage sheltered many flourishing velvet weavers during the eighteenth century. Next door are to be seen the Ragged

Schools and Widows' Alms House of the Parish of St John. Adjoining this is the railed frontage of Deanery Court.

Near the Harding Home can be seen the entrance to Copper Alley, within earshot of the ghostly reverberations of the rolling choruses of Handel's majestic *Messiah*. The oratorio was first performed at the Fishamble Street Musick Hall on 13 April 1742. This was what we would nowadays call a 'benefit' performance for the relief of the prisoners in the several gaols and 'for the support of Mercer's Hospital'. In 1777 the parking regulations for patrons of the theatre stated that they should be set down with the horses' heads towards Fishamble Street and be taken up with the horses facing Essex Street.

Plate 6. This picture, taken from the upstairs window of a house - recently demolished - on the south-western corner of Copper Alley, shows the courtyard and former Deanery of Christ Church Cathedral. It was built during the first half of the eighteenth century mainly on the site (and slightly to the south-east) of its seventeenth-century predecessor, traces of which were discovered during the

Plate 6. Photographer unknown. Georgian Society Records.

archaeological excavations here in the early 1970s. These included valuted cellars of small Dutch-like red brick. The Deanery was used by the cathedral until 1770, after which time it went through several changes until finally, in 1842 - as the date painted on the keystone of the arched entrance shows - it became St John's Parochial School. Subsequently, the parishes of St Nicholas Within and St Audoen were united by an order of the Privy Council in 1867. St Michael's, which was still in use in 1868 - according to the Royal Commission of that year - closed soon after to allow the beginning of the restoration of Christ Church in 1871. In 1877 the parishes of St Werburgh and St John were joined together and the latter's church closed in 1878. The plaques to be seen between the windows on the first storey bear the names St Audoen, St Nicholas, St Michael, St Werburgh, St John, thereby giving reason for the inscription 'United National Schools' on the string-course above the rusticated architraves of the ground floor. These features are in sharp contrast to the 'regular pediments', both triangular and segmental, used over the first-floor windows.

This was the last building on the western side of Fishamble Street. It abutted onto St John's Church to the south of which, across the lane, lay the cathedral. This portion of the street was considered as forming part of 'Bothe Street' or 'Boothe Street' because originally it had been occupied by a series of booths or shops which in the fourteenth century we find termed 'bothes'. This term has a meaning similar to 'shambles' and as late as 1630 the Proceedings of the Privy Council describe the stalls occupied by the fish-vendors here not as houses, but as 'voyde buildings' or booths. Maud Gonne-McBride, Yeats's 'Helen of social welfare dream', helped dispense fourpenny dinners from the school in 1911.

Plate 7. The house to the right of the entrance to Deanery Court in the middle of the eighteenth century was the home of an apothecary named Johnson who, Barrington tells us, 'procured a diploma as physician to make the family genteeler. He was a decent, orderly, good kind of apothecary, and a very respectable, though somewhat ostentatious, doctor, and, above all, a good orthodox, hard-praying Protestant'.

St John's Church just prior to its demolition in 1884 is shown here in the only known extant photograph of it. This is the Ensor rebuilding of 1766-9 and the order appears to be Ionic, but this is not clearly corroborated by the view of the church given in *The Gentlemen's Magazine* for 1786. The first church on this site, dating from the twelfth century, was enlarged in 1350. It was rebuilt about the year 1544 by Arland Ussher, and by 1589 appeals were being made for 'enlargement of the quyere'; in 1630 the church was said to have been still in 'good reparation' and a spire was added nine years later, but this merely advanced the decay which necessitated a new building in 1680-2. One of Dublin's saddest losses occurred at this time. The builders, Samuel Rothery and Michael Cook, were bound under the terms of their contract to take down carefully all the ancient monuments in the old church. Sadly, no provision was made for their reinstatement and, although these monuments have disappeared, many carved medieval grave slabs must lie deep in the churchyard. One relic of the medieval church is a breviary still to be seen in the library of Trinity College.

In July 1746 Henry Grattan, leader of the movement that forced Britain to grant legislative independence to Ireland in 1782 and later leader of the opposition to

Plate 7. Photographer unknown. Courtesy Guinness Hop Store collection.

the Union of England and Ireland, was baptised in St John's. In 1805 he was elected to the English House of Commons, where, until his death in June 1820, he campaigned for Catholic Emancipation.

St John's is the last resting place of over 12,500 departed citizens of Dublin. Among them is the wretched John Atherton, Bishop of Waterford and Lismore, hanged on Gallows Green for incest and other illicit offences, along with his man John Childe 'with whom he had committed the most foul crimes'. On the night of his execution, 6 December 1640, he was interred 'according to his desire in the remotest or obscurest part of the yard belonging to St John's Church'. The most famous of all Dublin fishmongers, Molly Malone, was laid to rest in St John's in 1734. The last burial, that of Miss Elizabeth McCausland, took place here in 1850.

Plate 8. Photograph attributed to Thomas F. Geoghegan. Courtesy L. O'Connor collection.

Plate 8. These two early, though much-altered, gabled houses of about 1692 stood on Wood Quay at the foot of Fishamble Street, near the site of Fyan's Castle and adjacent to the landing point known as the Fish Slip. The wall on the left is that of Essex Quay which was once fronted with triangular-gabled houses such as these with flush-sash windows, corner fireplaces, long narrow dark hallways and string courses. In this case the once-massive common central chimney stack has crumbled. In 1869 the house on the right was occupied by Edward Richardson, trunk manufacturer. In the foreground can be seen one of the ward's fire-escape ladders.

Fyan's Castle was a four-storey square tower, 38 feet by 20 feet. The walls were 4 feet in thickness and in 1585 were described as 'forty-towe foote hie'. John Fyan, who once occupied the tower house, was Mayor of Dublin in 1472 and again in 1479 and the family were prosperous merchants throughout the 1500s. Richard Fyan, Mayor in 1549 and 1564, was chiefly renowned for his hospitality. In the next century the tower became the property, by inheritance, of George Proudfoot, merchant, and it assumed his name. He was related to the Sheriff and during the years following the Restoration of Charles II 'Proudfoot's Castle' was used, on and off, as a state prison. In 1974 the massive foundations of this building were discovered and a sewer pipe was laid through them.

Running off to the right of the picture is Isod's Lane which, during the medieval period, led to Isolde's Tower and was a continuation of Scarlet Lane. This thoroughfare was later known as Blind Quay, as it was not on the river, and since 1776 has been called Lower Exchange Street.

Plate 9. A rare view of Wood Quay around 1900. An integral part of the Dublin Quays in their final stage of linear development. This was begun in the 1670s by Humphrey Jervis, with Ormonde's encouragement, and later punctuated by Cooley and Gandon's Four Courts and the latter's Custom House. Christ Church was always recognised as the dominant architectural feature of the ancient city built on the hill overlooking the old town. The Quay extended from The Crane at the foot of Winetavern Street to Isolde's Tower. That this was a wealthy area in the late seventeenth century is instanced by the fact that Christopher Lovett, Lord Mayor in 1676 and grandfather of Sir Edward Lovett Pearce, paid tax on a house of six hearths.

The building on the extreme right in the photograph was number 4, a Wyatt-windowed house of about 1815, housing Groves & Co's bookselling establishment, a trade shared with William Magee at number 5 next door. The more ornate front beyond the woman and child was appropriately the premises of Joseph Fagan, painter and decorator, who occupied numbers 13 and 14.

Here in number 14 once lived Denis Lambert Redmond who burned five tons of coal in a bonfire every 14 July since 1789 when the Parish Bastille, a symbol of royal tyranny to the French, was captured by an armed mob of Parisians during the French Revolution. In 1798 Redmond sheltered Myles Byrne and other Wexford men in his Wood Quay home. He was taken to Newgate and tortured; there he persuaded his prospective mother-in-law to smuggle in a pistol with which he made an attempt on his life. He asked to be buried beside Emmet in

Plate 9. Photographer: Thomas H. Mason. Courtesy National Library of Ireland.

Bully's Acre, one of the many supposed burial places of the patriot. His last (undelivered) letter to his finacée Henrietta Hatchall of number 1 Ormond Quay is to be seen in the State Paper Office. Denis Lambert Redmond was hanged outside his own door at Wood Quay on 6 October 1803.

The building adjoining Fagan's lay between the passages known as Redmond's Alley and Marshall Alley and housed, until its demolition in 1968, the Corporation Cleansing Department.

To the left of the picture, in the background, can be seen the pair of houses shown in the last photograph, that on the left here rebuilt as the photographic studio of Thomas F. Geoghegan, a leading professional who was official photographer to the National Gallery, and who moved here from number 6 Lower Sackville Street. From these windows he witnessed the setting up of guns on Wood Quay preparatory to the shelling of the Four Courts in 1922.

Plate 10. This remarkable exterior is probably the best remembered of all Wood Quay's recent buildings. Here at numbers 1 and 2 was Patrick Gaynor, vintner and tobacconist, in 1869. In the following year Mr John O'Connor became the proprietor of these premises and, in a last flourish of the Dublin stuccodores' art, executed on his behalf by two outstanding craftsmen, Messrs Burnet and Comerford, The Irish House took form; in C. P. Curran's words: 'its whole frontal all-glowing in colour like a Byzantine casket'. Over the door was O'Connor's escutcheon but successive proprietors also proudly painted their names on the front. Patrick O'Kelly, who resided nearby at number 13 Merchant's Quay, took over in 1879 and it became Charlie Dowling's in 1894, when The Irish House first receives mention – alongside Purcell's, the well known tobacconists, at number 3 – in Thom's Directory. In 1913 P. J. Dwyer came on the scene and from 1926 until 1942 it was known as Cleary's, then as Timoney's, until finally in 1945 James O'Meara's name went up over the door to await the march of municipal progress.

The framework of panels and inlaid pilasters was of the finest Portland cement, and the main figured panels displayed unashamed patriotic associations. One, entitled: 'Rich and rare were the gems she wore', taking its cue from Moore, depicted a maiden standing by a seated harpist. The most prominent tableau was that representing Grattan's last appeal in the Irish House of Commons before the passing of the Union. In another, 'Erin' was shown weeping on her stringless harp, lamenting the loss of her parliament and alongside was a fine, almost lifesize, O'Connell. As can be seen, the oak-panelled doors bore carved ringed celtic crosses; the interior was no less impressive, with oil paintings of the Vale of Avoca and the lakes of Killarney, along with a clock encased in a harp of Irish oak. The whole was crowned with a series of six round towers connected by a wrought-iron balustrade bearing the legends: 'Céad Míle Fáilte', 'Érin go bragh' and the date 1870. The niches contained representations of methers, harps, wolfhounds and the inauguration chair of the O'Neills of Clandeboy.

This photograph, taken on 24 June 1964, also shows part of number 3 Wood Quay: Fenning's record shop, the successor to Thomas J. Fenning's first store which opened here in 1918 and where he began trading as a 'general dealer'.

Plate 11. Winetavern Street as it was in the mid 1940s, showing the harmonious relationship between its buildings and Christ Church: a splendid evocation of

Plate 10. Photographer: Kevin Raynor. Courtesy Guinness Archive.

what a towering and powerful closure to this vista the cathedral really is. All these buildings, including the north face of Holy Trinity, were nineteenth-century work and retained a scale of streetscape which had its roots in the medieval period.

In 1195 the King's Gate, punctuating the city wall as it straddled Winetavern Street south of the junction with Cook Street, was named as a memorial to the accession of Richard I. Six years earlier the Lion-Heart of England had succeeded to the throne on the death of his father, Henry II, and spent all but six months of his ten-year reign in foreign battles. When he returned to England in 1194, after his imprisonment by Leopold of Austria, he was crowned for a second time, so Dubliners reaffirmed their loyalty in the dedication of the gate in Winetavern Street.

The ancient Great Guild Hall, where Dermot Mac Murrough's father was slain in 1120 and where the City Assembly once met, was sited on the eastern side of the street between the wall and John's Lane.

The famous Winetavern Street gunpowder explosion occurred near the bridge adjacent to Prickett's Tower and The Crane on 13 March 1597, when one hundred and forty-four barrels of powder were ignited by a spark and burst into flame. Over two hundred people were reported killed in the blast. 'It was not Winetavern Street alone that was destroyed on this occasion, but the next quarter of the town to it'.

But surely the most fascinating element is the street name itself, which encapsulates the history of inebriating liquors in Dublin from early medieval times. This *Vicus Tabernariorum Vini* was festooned with ale houses and taverns since the period when St Laurence O'Toole used to regale his guests with various kinds of wine. Mountjoy's secretary in the reign of Elizabeth I observed that when the native Irish 'come to any market towne to sell a cowe or a horse, they never returne home till they have drunke the price in Spanish wine (which they call the King of Spaine's daughter), or in Irish Usquebeagh'.

Barnaby Rych, responsible for the lines: '. . . it is a rare thing to find a house in Dublin without a taverne, as to find a taverne without a strumpet' is worth quoting

Plate 11. Photograph attributed to Wilkinson.

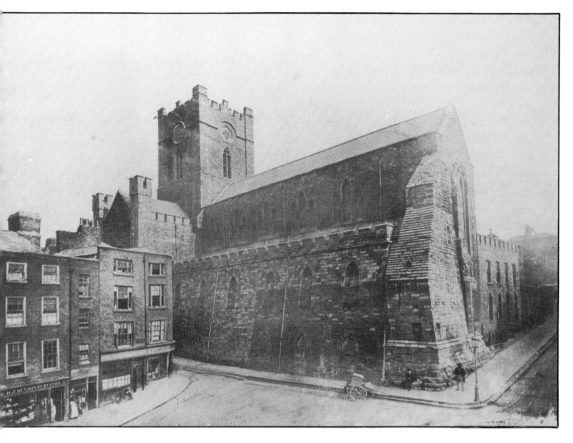

Plate 12. Photograph by Millard and Robinson. Courtesy J. R. W. Dick.

on the subject of wine taverns in Dublin during the reign of James I. At the time, (1624), any woman could lawfully either brew or sell ale. 'Let hir come from whence she will, if her credit will serve to borrowe a pan, and to buy but a measure of mault in the market, she setts uppe brewing . . . then they have a number of young ydle huswieves, that are both verie laothsome filthie and abominable, both in life and manners, and these they call taverne keepers, the most of them knowne harlots'.

The entrance to the yard of the Pyed Horse was through the gateway to be seen half way up on the left.

Let us spare a thought in this patchwork of memories for Thomas Tennant, a publican from Winetavern Street, who in 1770 was pilloried at the Tholsel for keeping a house of resort for journeymen tailors.

Plate 12. This dramatic pre-restoration photograph of Christ Church, taken from the north-west about 1870, demonstrates clearly the formidable task facing George Street, as well as underlining the liberties taken by him in the rebuilding of 1871-78. The stone buttressing on the north face with its blind arcading is truly massive, a reminder of the fall of the roof and south wall of the nave in 1562 along with the destruction of the south aisle and part of the west front.

Plate 13. Photographer: Norman Ashe. Courtesy E. C. Chandler.

Off to the left runs John's Lane, on the corner of which is to be seen number 1 Winetavern Street with its entrance neatly set at an angle and then occupied by John Lawlor, a provision dealer. Apart from the windows, a common feature shared with Messrs Kelly and Taylor 'engineers and machinists' at number 2, was the wide late-Georgian shopfront of c. 1800. Next door to these was what was popularly known as the narrowest house in Dublin, and having no number either in the photographs or the directories. It was a house of one bay, just over seven feet in width and three storeys high. In fact it appears to be no more than early-nineteenth-century infill between the comparatively late numbers 1 and 2 and the much earlier number 3, shown here with window sashes exposed and flush with the brickwork - after the fashion of the late-seventeenth and early-eighteenth century - rather than set in reveals. The sills were inserted at a later date. When the picture was taken D. J. Dundon, purveyor, was the occupier.

Following the passing of the Dublin Corporation Fire Brigade Act in June 1862 the position of Superintendent of the new Dublin Fire Brigade was given to Capt. Ingram, a Dubliner who had been a volunteer fireman in New York and London for some years. The brigade, consisting of twenty-four men, was set up in a new fire station in White Horse Yard, off Winetavern Street, where in 1863, for the first time in a European fire station, telegraphy was used to communicate with the second Dublin fire station in Coppinger's Row.

In 1621 the Rathbornes were making candles here not far from the Earl of Carlingford's mansion with its fourteen hearths. The Double Inn in Winetavern Street was one of Emmet's unused depots in 1803. Henry Hutton, Lord Mayor, resided at number 17 in 1804 and in 1812 Isaac Eaton, printer, published Shelley's 'An Address to the Irish People' here.

Built up against the south-west corner of the cathedral can be seen the battlemented exterior of the Verger's House as it appeared after the alterations of 1829-31. Just beyond this are the railings which were also a feature of this renovation and which followed the line of the north side of the newly-widened Skinners' Row. This work was carried out by the Wide Streets Commissioners in the early 1820s and the street was renamed Christchurch Place in 1833.

Plate 13. Christ Church again, from the north-west and from the air, but much altered. This postcard view published about 1949, from a fine crisp shot by Norman Ashe, shows the familiar flying buttresses and the baptistry added during the course of the late-nineteenth-century alterations. The house on the corner of John's Lane has gone and its neighbour, complete with that fine Georgian shopfront, was soon to go, along with its other companions then hopelessly shored up and waiting. In the midst of them all stands the little narrow house, half forgotten.

Along John's Lane can be seen the flat parapets on the old houses of the male choristers, with the Mission Hall beyond incorporating in its west gable end a part of St John's Church. Adjoining the hall is the churchyard; the area as it then existed gives a clear indication of the amount of interference which has taken place on this ancient burial site, particularly during 1977-8. The Jacobean Racquet Court is also plainly visible. Here is the very birthplace of Dublin, where the ramparts of the Viking *longphort* were originally thrown up as a stronghold in the tenth century. The remains of part of this fortification were revealed inside that section of the city wall first uncovered here in 1969.

CHAPTER 5

PATRICK F. WALLACE

A Reappraisal of the Archaeological Significance of Wood Quay

As more than three years have now (September 1984) elapsed since the completion of the Wood Quay/Fishamble Street excavations in 1981, it seems appropriate to review the archaeological significance of the site, especially as the interval since the conclusion of the work in the field has allowed of comparison of our findings by reference to the archaeological literature and recourse to foreign museums as well as discussions with international specialists. While continuing research may modify some of the conclusions tentatively advanced here, the present review at least has the merit of being based on the completed excavation programme and being undertaken after the director of the excavations has had sufficient time to stand back from the findings to assess them in broad international perspective. The present essay therefore supersedes an earlier attempt to review the archaeological significance of the site.[1] While not wishing to detract from the value of the earlier statement, the major points of significance which will be highlighted here differ in some respects both in essence and in slant from those made in 1979, not because the earlier summary was in any way wrong or intentionally misleading but rather because the great discoveries of the 1979-81 excavations were of such proportions that they altered previous impressions, gave rise to new ideas and generally made it necessary to rethink previous conclusions. It is hoped that the present reappraisal will be regarded as a 'post match' assessment in contrast with the earlier 'half time' comment, and that this does not preclude further appraisals according as the research and publication programme proceeds.

The major significance of the Wood Quay/Fishamble Street excavations must be their contribution to our understanding of the layout of tenth- and eleventh-century Dublin. Because such a large area was available for excavation, an 'open area' approach was decided on, whereby the emphasis was placed on uncovering the maximum area of ancient landscape, keeping the intrusion of baulks and section controls to the essential minimum. This approach allows the ancient topography to dictate and control the area and size of the area of excavation and contrasts with other excavation systems which sink in rigid pre-arranged spits or take place within a honeycomb of rectangular baulks which can obscure an overview of the original topography.

Ten plots or tenements of the Viking age were excavated along the Fishamble Street side of Wood Quay. This is the equivalent of one side of a street. Thanks to the remarkably good preservation of organic elements in these plots, it was

Above: View from riverside of second Viking-age embankment at Wood Quay.
Below: Section to show Dublin's encroachment into the bed of the Liffey between
the tenth and fourteenth centuries.

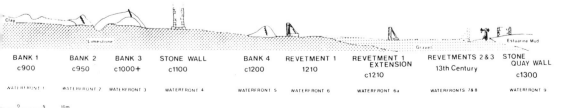

BANK 1	BANK 2	BANK 3	STONE WALL	BANK 4	REVETMENT 1	REVETMENT 1 EXTENSION	REVETMENTS 2 & 3	STONE QUAY WALL
c900	c950	c1000+	c1100	c1200	1210	c1210	13th Century	c1300
WATERFRONT 1	WATERFRONT 2	WATERFRONT 3	WATERFRONT 4	WATERFRONT 5	WATERFRONT 6	WATERFRONT 6a	WATERFRONTS 7 & 8	WATERFRONT 9

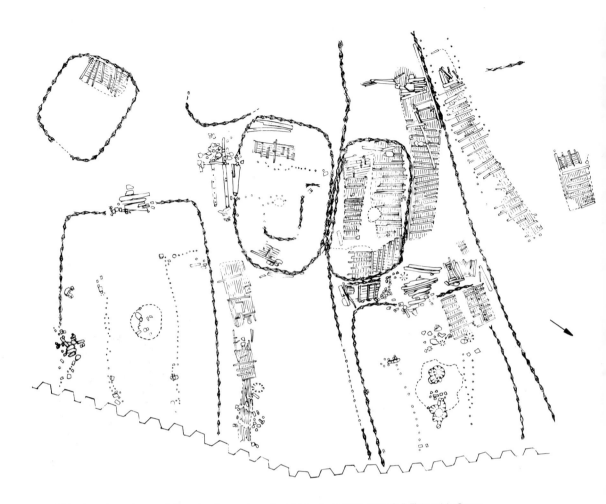

This plan shows house plots and pathways from the late tenth century, plots 2-5 Fishamble Street. Only the foundations remain; we see here remains of houses of Types 1 and 2. Woven wattle was used for pathways and inside the houses for floor mats.

possible in our 'open area' excavation not only to observe intact house foundations but also to see how the houses related to the plot boundaries, to other buildings, pathways and rubbish-pits within the individual plots. A whole townscape was uncovered and not just of one period but of as many as a dozen successive levels within the tenth- to eleventh-century period. The floors of the houses and the yards outside became higher all the time according as buildings were being rewalled and freshly thatched, as pathways were renewed and as rubbish and occupation debris were trampled under foot. By the time a house became obsolete and was due to be demolished its floor level was often 20cm higher than when the building was first occupied. When the old building was knocked and removed, the foundation was left behind. Thanks to the damp climate, and the wet anaerobic conditions into which pathways and foundations were often depressed, the foundations are often perfectly preserved along with the bedding material and occupation trample. Successive house foundations are often preserved like layered carpets of time, one on top of the other. So good

Tenth-century house foundations at Fishamble Street (in course of excavation, February, 1981).

was the preservation of organic remains at Wood Quay, that some of the bedding materials occasionally still preserved their original green colours.

To return to the town layout, it was established that the individual plots were mostly of trapezoidal shape with their widest end fronting onto what is presumed to have been the original Fishamble Street and their narrowest end near the earthen embankment which defended the town at the waterfront. The continuity of the boundary lines of these plots is most significant. Apart from one shift (possibly related to the slight expansion of the town towards the river with the erection of a second large defensive embankment), the lines of the properties or plots remained consistent throughout the tenth and the eleventh centuries. While the post-Norman/medieval plot levels did not survive – and it is therefore impossible to speak confidently of the continuity of plot boundaries from the Viking into the Norman period – such an inheritance can be postulated from the direction of property lines even as late as the eighteenth century by reference of Rocque's map of the area. The implication of the continuity of the lines of the Viking-age properties is that they are the products of an ordered urbanised society in which property was respected and its regulation possibly controlled by the legal force of an urban authority. It is impossible for the archaeologist to go any further than this but the town layout of Fishamble Street at least supplies the social historian and student of town planning with the stage on which to make further and more informed speculation.

In contrast with the apparently rigidly overseen plot control, it seems that a much greater freedom was allowed to the individual plot owner within the area of the plot. The size, position and number of buildings within the plot varied from plot to plot and from one level to the next. The only consistent characteristics noted within the plots were the invariable location of the long axis of the main building parallel to the length of the plot with the end of the house facing the end of the plot (and presumably the street) and secondly, the consistent provision of an individual access through each plot. It seems as though the provision of a woven wattle, log or stone-paved pathway in each plot was mandatory. Houses which spanned the whole width of a plot had to have doors at each end. It is possible that access to such pathways was at the discretion of the individual plot owners. Although of low proportions, plot boundary fences appear not to have been broken by gateways, the inference being that it was not usual (or not encouraged/expected/or even permitted?) to cross from one plot to the next other than by using the pathway (from the street?) to the streetward entrance of the main dwelling. Again, it is impossible to be sure whether many of these inferences are the result of the imposition of law or of the force of tradition and practice. That we are not simply speaking any longer just about the physical make-up of the town and its buildings, businesses, environment and economy but about the layout and use of property as well as of concepts like access, tradition and authority is, for me, the major significance of the Wood Quay excavation results. The closer the physical layout of the townscape brings us to the mentality of its occupiers the better. The environmental remains are also of assistance in this respect and will be discussed *infra*.

Turning to the physical make-up of the town, our most significant discoveries derive from the excellently preserved foundation layers of the Fishamble-Street buildings. Scores of intact foundations have been excavated and recorded. Coupled with Breandán Ó Ríordáin's earlier excavations of Dublin Viking-age buildings at High Street, Winetavern Street and Christchurch Place it is now possible to be confident about Dublin's basic building traditions and house types.[2] Four main house forms have been indentified.[3] All are rectangular in plan, most appear to be hip-roofed rather than gabled and nearly all must have been thatched. The principal building form, my *Type One,* was a rectangular structure about 8.50m long by about 4.75m wide. The wall was usually low (about 1.25m high) and almost always of post-and-wattle construction. The roof was supported on four main posts or groups of posts arranged in a rectangle within the floor area. The large door-jambs at the almost invariable endwall entrances also appear to have played a part in supporting the roof. Hand-in-hand with this roof-support system went a three-fold subdivision of the floor space. The widest strip stretched down the middle of the floor between the endwall entrances. This was often paved, gravelled or simply consisted of mud and trampled litter. A rectangular stone-kerbed fireplace was located in the centre. Presumably, there would have been a smokehole in the roof overhead. These buildings appear never to have been provided with chimneys. Along the side walls, two areas raised of turves and brushwood formed benches which also served as beds. The buildings were of open-plan design; sometimes corner areas near the doorways were partitioned off and provided with separate entrances in order to provide greater privacy.

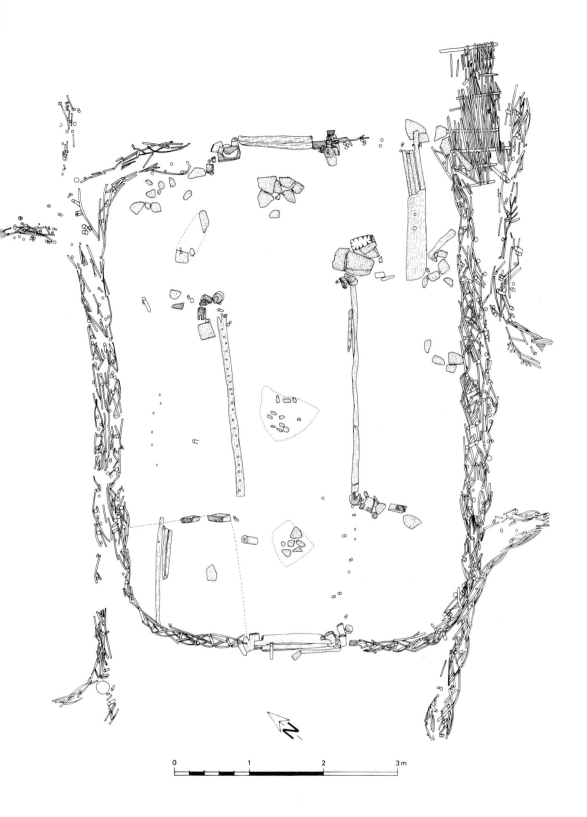

0   1   2   3 m

This shows the plan of the surviving foundation remains of a post
and wattle walled house of the eleventh century, Fishamble Street.

Above: Stone wall, erected about 1100, demarcating the line of the late Hiberno-Norse town along the riverside.

Below: This carved wooden hemisphere is reputed to be part of a native Irish High Cross and was found at Fishamble Street/Wood Quay.

The second main building form, *Type Two,* is smaller and apparently less draughty than the first type. It often has only a single entrance and this usually in the less windy southern side wall. There is a greater accent on comfort and usually these buildings have a proportionally greater floor area covered with organic bedding material than the *Type One* buildings in which the wide central floor strip was devoted to cooking, light industrial and craft pursuits. The smaller buildings usually measure less than 5m in length and about 3.75m in width. Although they are provided with lateral access, their roof-floor axis is longitudinal like the larger *Type One* buildings to which the arrangement of the roof supports is identical. It is possible that the smaller buildings represent the housing under a separate roof of a function previously contained within the larger (*Type One*) building, possibly the corner compartment area.

Dublin's third building form, *Type Three,* appears to have been a semi-underground building of which no example was found in Fishamble Street. Mr Ó Ríordáin excavated two examples of such a building in Winetavern Street. While these can hardly relate to the *grubenhaus* which is found in Germany, Scandinavia and England but not in Ireland, it is possible that it relates to the native Irish underground storage structure known as the *souterrain.* Unlike *Types One* and *Two* which were primarily built for human habitation, *Type Three* almost certainly was not. The only other Dublin Viking-age building group known to date, *Type Four,* consists of a series of small rectangular hut-like sheds which were probably for storage. Only a few of these have been found. In Fishamble Street, they tended to be located at the riverward end of the plots, that is nearer the waterfront than the main dwellings.

Apart from the information provided on house form and building type, the Wood Quay/Fishamble Street excavations have provided considerable data on construction methods and building fashions. In regard to the latter, certain architectural details such as wooden floors, grooved sole-plates for vertical revetment planks etc., appear to be common at certain levels and not at others. A marked improvement in the carpentry skills used in housing was detected in the later eleventh century.[4] This may have been related to the Hibernicisation of the town at a period from which it was politically dominated by Irish kings — the famous series of 'Kings with opposition' of the later eleventh and early twelfth centuries.

After the evidence for the town layout and the building information, the third most significant aspect of the Wood Quay excavations is the light they shed on Dublin's Viking-age and Anglo-Norman waterfronts. Nine successive stages by which the river Liffey was embanked have been identified.[5] In the period between the tenth and early fourteenth centuries about 80m was reclaimed from the bed of the river at Wood Quay. Starting with the earliest flood banks built above the high-water mark to keep dry the properties of the tenth-century town, the Vikings then built a defensive embankment topped with a post-and-wattle palisade. This was replaced by a larger embankment which presumably, like its predecessor, encircled the whole later Viking-age town. The larger bank was topped with a stave-built palisade behind which the defenders of eleventh-century Dublin would probably have crouched. Somewhat later a stone wall was erected. This was Dublin's first stone wall and it too probably encircled the town. It fell into disuse with the arrival of the Normans and their great expansion of the port area. Their initial advance on the bed of the Liffey seems to have been to erect a short-lived breakwater. This was followed around 1210 by the erection of a long front-braced vertical waterfront revetment wall. This wooden wall or dockside was built in a number of sections, each section probably being the creation of the individual burgess whose property extended onto the particular shore area. Careful recording of these wooden structures has revolutionised our knowledge of Ireland's medieval carpentry. These wooden revetments appear to have been constructed to accommodate docking ships in a port which even in the medieval period was notorious for its shallowness.[6] Indeed, it was probably the increased size of Norman-period and later ships, the increased trade of the thirteenth-century boom period and the desire to increase the draught of water at Dublin's port which led to the building of these massive revetment walls.

In all, three roughly parallel wooden revetments were built approximately in succession of one another along Wood Quay in the thirteenth century. The last one was back braced, the earlier ones being braced from the riverward side. Our excavations also uncovered the possibly early fourteenth-century stone quay wall which succeeded the wooden revetments. In contrast with the multi-layered habitation remains – the buildings and pathways of the Viking-age – the thirteenth-century waterfronts provided a totally different kind of evidence and demanded a different excavation approach. Unlike the gradually accumulated habitation layers of the tenth and eleventh centuries, and even of the Viking-age banks which were built of dump construction, the thirteenth-century waterfronts were backed by tons of gravel, estuarine mud and redeposited urban refuse all combined to reclaim a very large waterfront reception area behind the wooden dock walls. The scale of this engineering is massive and impressive, even by modern standards.

No less than the significance of the discovery of well-preserved waterlogged wood for the study of engineering and carpentry traditions of the Viking-age as already discussed, the Wood Quay site has also increased our knowledge of thirteenth-century carpentry.[7] This is especially significant for a country which, in contrast to most of its European neighbours, has very little by way of surviving medieval timber in any of the relevant standing buildings. Now, thanks to the waterfront timbers, we have a whole compendium of the joints favoured by thirteenth-century Dublin carpenters. Even more significantly, it is also possible now to make comparisons between this carpentry and that of the preceeding Viking-age and the even earlier indigenous traditions preserved in the horizontal mills, and to tentatively fit the impressions of such comparisons to historical periods and watersheds. For instance, comparison of the carpentry traditions of the periods before and after the arrival in Dublin of the Normans allows of the tentative conclusion that the thirteenth-century waterfronts which were probably commissioned by the new masters of Dublin were built by men working in the indigenous local tradition, a conclusion which can be taken to support the idea that the Normans probably retained native Dublin craftsmen and that not all the original Hiberno-Norse population was banished to Oxmanstown after the Norman takeover of the town. The probability of the Normans introducing superior carpentry joints and building methods which were probably lavished on military and ecclesiastical buildings has also to be borne in mind as it is likely that such a tradition coexisted alongside the indigenous craft as preserved in the waterfront revetments.

The next most significant result of the Wood Quay excavations must be the information they shed on the various crafts practised in the Viking and Norman period town. Despite the apparently basic quality of the carpentry employed in the buildings of the Viking-age town, other extremely skilful craftsmen also worked on wood. Among these were coopers, turners, shipwrights and carvers, all of whose products are preserved in Dublin's waterlogged conditions. Tree-ring studies of thirteenth-century waterfront timbers, incorporating re-used ships' planks, suggest that the planks come from ships built in late twelfth-century Ireland.[8] It is also possible that some of the ships represented among the *detritus* of the earlier period were repaired if not built in Dublin. When published, Dr Seán McGrail's report on the thirteenth-century ships' timbers from Wood Quay will have far-reaching impact, as ships of this period are not common in Western Europe. For example, the only two mast-crutches or *mykes* known at present were found at Wood Quay. As with other crafts it will be interesting to see if there is much continuity of craft tradition in the eventual comparison of the Viking-age and Anglo-Norman ships' timbers.

The work of the cooper survives in the numerous staves and hoops which have been found. The staves appear to resemble those of the more modern cooper whereas the hoops are usually made of split saplings which are fastened by means of an iron clip or a notched terminal threaded through a slit in the other terminal. The pole-lathe appears to have been used by turners to produce bowls, ladles and plates. Turners also probably produced other single-piece wooden articles like kegs, lossets, chutes, handles, gaming-pieces and gaming boards, spindles, weavers' swords, etc. Sometimes these artifacts of everyday life are decorated in a rustic or folk-art style comprised of pendant triangles, criss-crosses and other rectilinear arrangements. Objects decorated in a high-art style have also been found in the excavations.

The outstanding series of wooden ornaments carved in the eleventh-century Hiberno-Norse *Ringerike* style, which have been recovered in the Wood Quay/Fishamble Street excavations, are significant for two principal reasons – apart from their intrinsic beauty as wooden *objets d'art*. Firstly, they clearly demonstrate that great art was not simply confined to metal and stone – the two materials in which it normally survives – but rather that the art of objects like the famous crozier shrines and other reliquaries were matched by richly decorated carved wooden objects. Secondly, the confidence and individuality of Dublin's *Ringerike* style as we now know it from this carved wooden series, and the sheer volume of the material, seriously questions the extent of the Scandinavian contribution to insular *Ringerike* and rather seems to suggest that the insular contribution to the origins and character of the Dublin school has been underemphasised. The volume and perfection of this style as interpreted by Dublin's wood carvers, together with the evidence for metalworking and the discovery of so many trial-pieces in another part of the town raise the possibility of many eleventh-century pieces of Irish Christian metalwork having been produced in later Viking-age Dublin *ateliers*. When published, Mr James Lang's report on the decorated carved wood from Wood Quay/Fishamble Street will

Above: Wooden quayside revetment of early thirteenth century at Wood Quay.

Below: Runic Inscription, part of which has been read as 'Deer's Horn . . .' from Wood Quay/Fishamble Street.

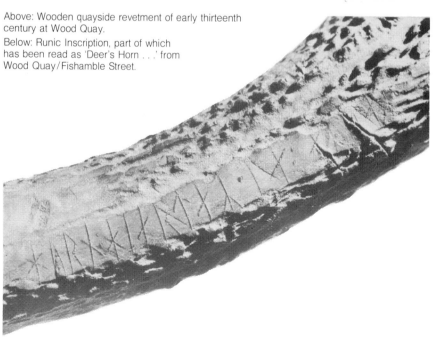

make a significant contribution to Viking-age art studies. In respect of the carved wood *corpus,* it is also significant that our first tangible evidence for the possibility of the Irish High Cross having been also produced in wooden versions or having had wooden prototypes has come in the form of a wooden hemisphere carved with interlaced bands which was recovered from a tenth-century house foundation layer in Fishamble Street. By analogy with surviving stone crosses at sites like Clogher and Tynan in southern Ulster, this object is best regarded as a boss which was pegged to the front of a wooden cross at the junction of the arms and shaft. How such tangible proof of Viking Dublin's contact with the native hinterland came to end up where it did is a matter for speculation.

Apart from the various woodworking crafts already mentioned, our excavations have also shed considerable light on other crafts and their products. Principal among these is the blacksmith, whose versatility and wide-ranging demand is well attested.[9] Not only did the smiths manufacture domestic fittings and implements, they made the tools for their own and most other crafts. The *corpus* of the iron tools, fittings, arms etc. from Wood Quay is enormous and will form one of the first reports of the projected publication programme. While it appears that many iron tools and fittings went unchanged from Celtic to modern times, there is no doubting the impact of the Viking blacksmith, whose superior skill at producing hard steel edges had been perfected in the course of the evolution of the fine swords, spearheads, arrowheads which had such impact on native weapons.[10] Presumably some of the new forging skills spread to the native population as rapidly as did the advantages of the new weapons. Dr Brian Scott's projected metallographic analysis of the Wood Quay iron of both the Viking and Anglo-Norman periods will allow of more constructive conclusions about the degree to which the products of the smiths of the tenth to the thirteenth centuries were innovative or derived of an indigenous tradition, as appears to have been the case with the carpentry.

Among the non-ferrous metalworkers were silversmiths and goldsmiths, bronzesmiths and leadsmiths. A small quantity of gold ornaments has been recovered while considerable numbers of copper-alloy products, such as tweezers, cloak pins of both the plain stick and ringed pin type, as well as weighing scales and their pans, demonstrate the skill of the bronzesmith. The bone 'trial' or 'motif'-pieces which were so conspicuous in the Christchurch Place/High Street sites are scarce in Wood Quay/Fishamble Street which is somewhat away from the area of the town where the non-ferrous metalworking crafts appear to have been concentrated. These bones appear to have served both as surfaces on which apprentices copied the designs and motifs of master craftsmen and, in the case of the well-executed specimens, as models for depressing into sand or clay moulds or on which foil was shaped. Considerable evidence for the use of sheet lead and the casting of lead balance weights has also come to light.[11]

The production of bone and antler artifacts, especially of combs, spindle whorls, gaming-pieces, clamps etc., is well attested in Dublin. Although the main bone-working centre seems to have been concentrated in the High Street area, several combs and other bone and antler products have been recovered from Fishamble Street. Similarly, while many leather artifacts have been recovered from the Wood Quay area, their main centre of production also appears to have been near the High Street area. Apart from *Ringerike* decorated sword scabbards of the Viking-age, a very important series of decorated knife-sheaths of the thirteenth century has been recovered from the waterfront site at Wood Quay. Two parts of what have been taken to be a rare early thirteenth-century French leather book cover have been identified by Mr Joseph McDonnell, whose report is awaited.

One of the most significant craftsmen's workshops to have been excavated anywhere must be the succession of amberworkers' houses in one of the Fishamble Street plots where broken and discarded amber beads and rings as well as discarded waste chips were strewn on the floors of a succession of houses in Plot 2. Conspicuous among the products of this workshop were hemispherical and trapezoidal beads, cruciform-shaped pendants and finger rings. The greatest difficulty in the production of this range of amber jewellery appears to have been to make a perforation without splitting the bead, pendant or ring. Hundreds of discarded broken pieces appear to be casualties of poor perforation tools. The amber itself had to be imported in nodules from the Baltic coastlands or from East England. The latter coast also yielded jet, which was turned into bracelets and which appear to have been produced in the amberworking house. Glass beads also appear to have been produced in Viking Dublin, to judge from the number of hemispherical glass drops which solidified on contemporary house floors. Broken glass vessels may have been specially imported to supply local glass-bead production.

Turning to the archaeological evidence for international trade, we find that pottery is the surviving artifact most eloquent of Dublin's trade of both the Viking and Anglo-Norman ages. A very general summary statement has already been made on the voluminous *corpus* of pottery evidence from Wood Quay[12] and further articles are about to appear.[13] Cooking pots of English (especially Chester) origin have turned up from tenth-century levels. Glazed pots were imported from Late Saxon England and, in the later eleventh century, Normandy red-painted and Andennes vessels. Conspicuous among this assemblage is a pair of lidded jugs of probable French origin. It was not until the later twelfth century that Dublin produced its own pottery. Dublin-made jugs and storage vessels are very common among the thousands of sherds recovered from the infill dumped behind the thirteenth-century revetments. Pottery continued to be imported with products of the kilns of Bristol, Chester, Gloucester being the most numerous English imports. The French trade continued with fine quality wine jugs coming from the Saintonge area through the port of Bordeaux and mortars also originating in Western France. Apart from the ubiquitous green glazed Saintonge vessels, South-Western France also produced polychromes which are found in Dublin. Rouen and the Paris area also produced fine pottery which turns up at Wood Quay. We have been fortunate also to find a series of painted pottery sherds of Mediterranean origin as well as *archaic majolica* and other rare imports at Wood Quay. Fragments of rare ceramic trumpets of Saintonge origin have also been found. A series of blue-grey 'Paffrath' skillets indicate trade links with the Rhineland but the dominance of the English and French trade connections has to be admitted. Even small amounts of late-medieval and post-medieval potsherds and clay-pipes have been found on the Wood Quay site. Among the most important discoveries of pottery must be the few so-called *souterrain* vessels of native manufacture which were found in late eleventh- and early twelfth-century contexts. This was the only native ware produced in early medieval Ireland and as its area of production tended to be confined to the north-east, its discovery at Wood Quay indicates some kind of trade or exchange contact with Ulster.

As has been seen in respect of the summaries of other discoveries at Wood Quay, the historical implications of the pottery are at least as important as the intrinsic significance of the vessels themselves. Of all the surviving imported artifacts, pottery is the best barometer of Dublin's trade network. Progressing from the tenth- and eleventh-century links with England, we find that pottery comes in from France after the Norman Conquest of England in 1066. The discovery of pottery of French origin in Dublin before the arrival of the Normans here, suggests that trade contacts were already strong between Dublin and the Norman world before 1170, especially if the pottery trade is reflective of the more voluminous and lucrative wine trade.

Apart from pottery, amber and jet, other definite imports of the Viking-age include finished soapstone vessels from the North Atlantic area and walrus ivory from the Arctic. The fine quality worsteds which have been found were probably imported from England. The silk kerchiefs, silk caps and silk ribbons which have been found in a relatively good state of preservation probably originated in the East Mediterranean area. A silk-backed piece of woven gold braid may have come from even farther afield. Apart from such obvious imports there is also other evidence of foreign contacts: porphyry tiles brought as pilgrims' souvenirs from eleventh-century Rome, *terra sigillata* brought as a possible medicinal compound from eleventh-century France, carved Saxon ivories from England, a gold ring with a garnet inset of Germanic origin, and, in the Norman period, a series of tiny pilgrims' flasks or *ampullae* brought from Canterbury and a pilgrims' badge from an unknown shrine.

Archaeological discoveries of exotic nature at Wood Quay confirm Dublin's economic importance in the later Viking-age when it dominated the Irish Sea area and was one of the great ports of Western Europe. The discovery of so many silver hoards of ninth- and tenth-century date in Ireland testifies to the richness of contemporary trade. It is likely that much of this imported silver was mediated through the port of Dublin. Dolley has shown that Dublin's first mint was established in or about 997.[14] The first coins to be minted were clearly based on English prototypes and were originally intended for use in English ports where Dublin's currency was accepted until after the first quarter of the eleventh century. Thanks to the discovery of a remarkable series of tenth-century English coins not in a hoard nor a dispersed hoard but in different locations and at different levels over the Fishamble Street site, it is also clear now that coins were hoarded in Dublin for use in English trade long before the establishment of a local mint. This English series bears mint signatures of towns like Chester, Norwich, London, Exeter etc. A recent study of Dublin's more than two hundred and fifty lead weights shows a rigid adherence to the Carolingian ounce system as nearly all the weights appear to be multiples or fractions of a basic unit of 26.6

grammes.[15] Apart from the weights, a series of pans and scales and their components was also unearthed in the course of the excavations.

The limitations of archaeological evidence even from a site with such good preservation as Wood Quay have to be admitted. There are many imports, such as wine, for which we have to rely solely on the documentary evidence and it is impossible to know what Dublin's main exports were. Slaves and metalwork were much sought-after in the earlier Viking-age, Dublin's original principal *raison d'être* being a slave emporium. Hides, wool and cloth were probably among Dublin's principal exports in the later Viking-age. The town's income was supplemented by the hiring of its fleet for naval warfare and from the provisioning of ships on the lucrative north-south trade route on which it grew up. Ringed pins of Irish type have been found at sites like York and even on Viking sites in the North Atlantic area. These cannot be regarded as Irish or Dublin exports but rather as indications of the transmission of an Irish fashion along trade routes frequented by Vikings with recourse to Dublin.[16]

The importance of Dublin's close connection with Saxon England should not be underestimated, especially in economic terms. It has already been suggested that the origins of Dublin should be sought in the broad political and economic context of Ireland/the Irish Sea/Western England and not in Scandinavian terms.[17] More recently an attempt has been made to measure the continuing influences tenth- and eleventh-century Dublin received from Late Saxon England by reference to the archaeological discoveries at Wood Quay.[18] As has already been suggested, the early involvement of the Normans in Dublin may be derived of Dublin's earlier trade and ecclesiastical links with England and may be reflected on the ground by the discovery of so much Norman pottery long before the arrival of Strongbow and Henry II.

The measurement of native Irish influences in Viking Dublin is difficult by reference only to the archaeological evidence. Nevertheless, that there is considerable overlap in the material culture of sites like Ballinderry, Strokestown and Knowth on the one hand and Dublin on the other has to be admitted. It is hoped that some of the focus of future research will highlight possible native craft traditions in the Viking-age town. More information on native monastic layout and character, indigenous house types, building traditions and crafts will help place Dublin in a better perspective. Our discoveries certainly call for a reappraisal of some of the pioneering statements made largely from the historical side on the impact of the Vikings on Ireland.[19] The extent to which incoming groups like the Vikings or the Normans/English effected change in the material culture of Dublin is of absorbing interest. An earlier attempt[20] to gauge the extent of the Norman impact on the material culture of Dublin appears to have found some support from a historical quarter.[21]

Before concluding with an assessment of the significance of Wood Quay against foreign sites and of how our discoveries can be of assistance to local and international studies, it is important to note that a programme to publish the findings is now underway. A *corpus* of the buildings will be followed successively by reports on the various artifact groups — iron, wood, bone and antler, pottery, leather, stone etc. Further reports will deal with the waterfronts and the city wall, the pottery and the environmental evidence. Already Mr Vincent Butler has

Top: Stamped leather bookcover of North French (Paris?) origin. Early thirteenth century, Wood Quay.

Above: This English nummular brooch was found in a later tenth-century context at Fishamble Street/Wood Quay.

Right: Detail of wooden finial with openwork design carved in Dublin's eleventh-century Hiberno-Norse Ringerike style. From Fishamble Street/Wood Quay.

prepared a thesis on the thirteenth-century cattle bones. His projected plan will continue with a study of the other thirteenth-century animal bones and concentrate finally on the animal bones of Viking Dublin. His findings will amplify our knowledge of animal husbandry, diet and butchery and will add to the important impressions made in Mr Finbarr McCormick's pioneering work on the animal bones. Building on Professor G. F. Mitchell's work on the environmental remains, especially on the waterfront, Ms Siobhán Geraghty has concentrated on the macroscopic plant remains to learn more about the plant environment, economy and diet of the Viking town as well as more about the use of plants for industrial and building purposes. It is hoped that pollen and botanical analyses will also be undertaken as well as tree-ring dating of the many wooden samples taken from the various buildings. Ms Frances Pritchard's *corpus* of the textiles will also be awaited with interest, especially as it will include a section on some silk scarves which Ms Libby Heckett is preparing under her direction. General summaries of the archaeology of Viking-age[22] and Anglo-Norman Dublin[23] have already been made, a basic statement on social life in the Viking town has appeared[24] and a synthesis on the archaeology of Dublin is also nearing completion . The excavation of the Wood Quay/Fishamble Street site was the largest operation of its type undertaken in Ireland. It included a range of different sites — Viking urban, Viking waterfront and Anglo-Norman waterfront. The excellent preservation means that there is now a very large *cache* of artifacts and environmental samples in addition to an extensive archive on the structures which were excavated.

One of the most significant contributions of the Wood Quay evidence is that it also spotlights the deficiencies in our knowledge of early medieval Dublin and in so doing points to targets for future excavation and research. In our failure to find the earliest ninth-century *longphort* settlement, we have confirmed that this earliest Viking township at Dublin was located elsewhere and probably near the Islandbridge/Kilmainham cemetery which was discovered in the last century. Apart from the occasional discovery of a burial of the tenth- and eleventh-century period within the walled area of the Viking town at Wood Quay and of a collection of thirteenth-century burials at the riverward side of the wall, our excavations uncovered no trace of a cemetery for the Viking/Norman period town. Hopefully, future excavation in the right place will find such a cemetery, or ongoing research into known burial places (like Castleknock?) will identify the cemetery of the late Viking period. The absence of graveyards and the gradual Christianisation of the Dubliners by 1000 will not make this task easy. A number of elements of the tenth- and eleventh-century town also need elucidation. We have not found any place of worship or assembly, nor have we found the king's residence/palace/citadel. Also to be identified are the streets. From the layout and topography of both the tenth- and eleventh-century and later-period town we have assumed that much of the present street system originates in the Viking-age, especially down Fishamble Street from which the plots we excavated must have radiated. It is important that the actual streetways be found and their character, composition and relationship to the plots be mapped. The task will not be easy especially if our assumption that the ancient street network lies under the existing one is correct. It is also hoped that future work will unearth evidence for the extramural suburbs and the routeways which radiated from them to the hinterland and beyond. The absence of archaeological evidence for town layout and houses for the thirteenth and later centuries is a major drawback for students of urban continuity and the measurement of the impact of traditional planning and building practices on later development. It is hoped that good preservation and large 'open area' excavation of a townscape as uncovered at Wood Quay/Fishamble Street will attract the focus of social geographers and anthropologists who, being supplied with the environment and economy of tenth- and eleventh-century Dublin will use their expertise to speculate on family size, population, longevity, fertility and other sociological questions in order that we can come as close as possible to the people of a thousand years ago. Perhaps the most significant result of the archaeological discoveries at Wood Quay is the exciting realisation that we can now learn much more than would have been dreamed possible not even a generation ago. We are only at the beginning . . .

The archaeological findings at Wood Quay are significant in European terms because of the sheer scale of the site and the excellent preservation of materials made of organic substances like wood and leather which would have disintegrated in anything other than a waterlogged environment. It is not the thousands of artifacts of trade, craft and everyday life which are primarily significant in European terms. Rather it is the flood of light the site throws on the layout of an early medieval North-West European town in which native Irish, English and Scandinavian elements played a part. No other site has presented ten plots with as many as twelve successive houses one on top of the other as well as waterfront/defensive embankments of the tenth and eleventh centuries and a series of wooden dockside revetments of the thirteenth century. Some of the large English urban excavations like London and Chester have produced great evidence of the Roman period which we cannot match, others like Winchester have shed light on how Christian institutions were part of a Saxon town which had Roman origins, while work at York and Lincoln has told us much about urban life, craft and international trade in the tenth- and eleventh-century period. York and Dublin were linked dynastically in the Viking-age. In recent times both cities have had major archaeological excavations so it is hardly surprising that people make comparisons between the two towns even to the extent of comparing how their respective archaeologists fare at the hands of developers, in respect of funds to undertake post-excavation research and of how the results are presented to the public in museum displays. While comparison of the present situation is useful and may redound to the advantage of Dublin in respect of prompting the relevant authorities to capitalise on the local discoveries, comparison of the archaeological results and findings is much more exciting and will go on for a long time. There are general similarities in the town layout and in the nature of the enclosing embankments, but vast differences in building types and construction methods. There are both parallels and disparities in the respective groups of artifacts from the towns which will be subjects for future research.

In relation to the other great early medieval European urban sites, it has to be admitted that Wood Quay is significant not for the light it sheds on the origins of urbanisation because sites like Birka, Haithabu and Arhus have earlier layers but for its information on town layout, organisation and building at a period when the North European town had already evolved. It is significant rather as Novgorod is, although it lacks the late medieval evidence and continuity for which the Russian town is famous. The Trondheim and Oslo sites have produced valuable information on a town layout, the inception of which post-dates that of Dublin as well as on building types which are very different to those known from Wood Quay/Fishamble Street. Although later than North Sea ports like the as yet undiscovered Quentovik and less well preserved sites like Dorestad and Doredrecht, it appears to be coeval with the excavated evidence at Antwerp, the published information on which is available only in summary form. It is probably matched in terms of scale and preservation by southern Baltic sites like Railswick in the German Democratic Republic and Wolin in Poland, although more in the mainstream of the developing transalpine town than its Slavic contemporaries.

It is important to realise that Wood Quay is significant on a number of different levels. Apart from sites such as those which have been noted for their relevance to the development of the European medieval town, Wood Quay's wooden waterfronts of the High Middle Ages can be compared with those of the great waterfront excavation sites of Amsterdam, Bergen, London and King's Lynn while the volume and range of its thirteenth- and early fourteenth-century pottery compares with that of Southampton, its pre-Norman pottery being (to my knowledge) unmatched in its range and volume. The bone and combworking areas of Ribe, Arhus and Trondheim are parallelled by those of High Street Dublin, while Lund's range of decorated wood is matched by the Fishamble Street series. Unfortunately, York's evidence for minting is not matched in Dublin. While sites like York, Lincoln, Durham, Lund, Sigtuna, Arhus, Oslo, Trondheim, Haithabu, Antwerp etc. have shed considerable light on their respective building types and construction methods, the volume of well-preserved house foundations in Dublin (especially Fishamble Street) is unparalelled except in Eastern Europe.

In summary, Dublin and the Wood Quay results are significant for European urban studies, for what they teach about early town layout, defences, waterfronts, international trade networks as well as for artifact, economical and environmental studies. Its good preservation of structures makes it a key reference for reconstructions of ancient buildings or conclusions based on dry-site evidence only. The volume and range of the structures and artifacts and their evolution and production at a site where in varying degrees three ethnic groupings – Irish, Scandinavian and English – appear to have played different parts makes it an important site of which to ask general questions about European history, archaeology and development as well as questions about whether there is a common European material culture or ethnically identifiable artifacts or whether waves of material cultural influence spread in different directions at various times. Future publication, display and reconstruction of our Wood Quay structures and artifacts should be of benefit to our British and Continental colleagues, teachers, students and visitors.

The significance of the Wood Quay excavations in Irish terms can be summarised under archaeological, historical, academic and educational as well

Two views of a cal wooden figurine for in a late eleventh-century Fishamble Street house.

130

as economic and tourism considerations. In physical archaeological terms we now know more about the character and layout of Ireland's first town – still our capital city – than before. We now know a great deal about our ancient building forms and construction methods and we can use this information to elucidate problems of understanding dry-sites of native occupation as well as to make comparisons with our native quasi-urban settlements, the great monasteries. We can now, literally, envisage what Dublin was like at the time of Brian Boru and the Battle of Clontarf because we have found that the house foundations, pathways etc. of that time actually survive. We can witness the wealth of Dublin in real terms because of the surviving imported silks and other items of trade. The range of tools and everyday things which have been found enable us to piece together the everyday life of various craftsmen, not least the carpenter about whom we

Three lead alloy pilgrim's flasks or ampullae brought from Canterbury to Dublin in the early thirteenth century. They commemorate Thomas a'Becket and were all found at Wood Quay.

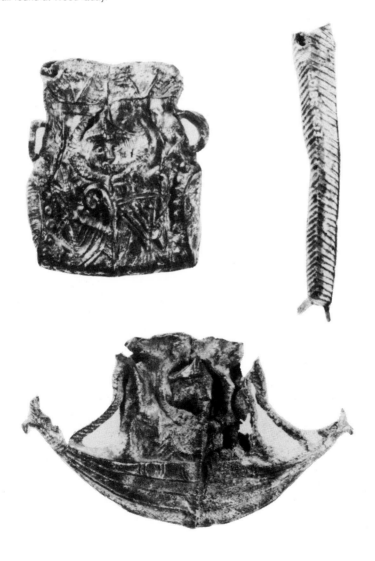

previously knew so little. Thanks to the animal bone and environmental remains and the analyses to which they are being subjected, we will know about nutrition, sanitation, diet, economy, animal types etc. and, despite the relative absence of historical information on social and economic topics for this period, we should eventually know as much about the Dublin of Brian Boru's time as we do of that of Swift's era.

Historical data will always have to be used to establish the correct balance and interpretation of our archaeological results as well as to fill in details about which archaeology is silent. Historical chestnuts like the impact of the Vikings, the longevity of Scandinavian influence, the relative wealth of eleventh-century Dublin, the extent of the English influence at the time of Harold, the degree to which Dublin was part of the Norman trading world before 1169, the influence of the 'men of Bristol' in Dublin after 1171, the degree to which the Norman invasion was a follow up on pre-existing trade patterns rather than a revolutionary change, and the extent to which the thirteenth century was a boom period are all qualified to varying degrees by the discoveries at Wood Quay and the other Dublin sites. It is perhaps significant that the scholar most associated with the campaign to save the Wood Quay site for excavation is a historian, not an archaeologist. Sad to say that even in the debate about the importance of the site in the High Court, it was from the ranks of archaeologists that a couple of people were found to say that this site was unimportant. The visits of foreign scholars to Ireland and the greater realisation of the value of an interdisciplinary approach to the past has confirmed academic interest in the site. One of the best long-term results of the whole debate has been to secure a place for medieval and urban archaeology in university courses where once it might have been regarded as 'too recent' or 'too foreign' for inclusion. Now that questions about the site and its significance appear in examinations, it may finally be said to have 'arrived'. This process should accelerate with the appearance of published results. It is also hoped that kindred aspects of Ireland's material culture – post-medieval and industrial archaeology as well as our material folk culture – will also find increasing academic recognition. Even more importantly, it is hoped that the present interest of primary and secondary school programmes in the results of work like this and their display in museums will escalate. Our physical heritage will be in a much healthier state of protection when the results of excavations such as that at Wood Quay percolate fully into schoolrooms and schoolbooks. Finally, there can be little doubt that a proper museum display and reconstruction of our discoveries, as well as related spin-off activities such as lectures, guided tours and popular books, would generate tourism and conference visitors which would be of economic benefit to Dublin.

I must conclude by paying tribute to the pioneering work of my predecessor, Mr A. B. Ó Ríordáin, whose spectacular excavations at High Street, Winetavern Street and especially at Christchurch Place were so significant. Rather than being in any way a repetition, the Wood Quay/Fishamble Street sites shed light on new aspects of the Viking/Norman town. I am grateful to successive Directors and Keepers of Irish Antiquities at the National Museum of Ireland for allowing me the privilege of conducting these excavations on behalf of that institution.

CHAPTER 6

BREANDÁN Ó RÍORDÁIN

Excavations in Old Dublin

One of the more comprehensive studies of the early phases of Dublin's history, Charles Haliday's *The Scandinavian Kingdom of Dublin,* first published in 1881, deals in some detail with the documentary evidence concerning the founding of Dublin in the ninth century, its rulers during the Viking period and its relationship with other Norse settlements. It also includes an essay, 'On the ancient name of Dublin'.[1] In this essay Haliday refers to the nature of the soil in the older parts of the city, e.g. High Street, Castle Street and Fishamble Street, and mentions the discovery of squared oak timbers, shells, leaves and other materials which came to light in the course of the laying of underground sewers in the city streets in the nineteenth century. Additional information on the finding of similar material of archaeological interest is contained in a diary written by Thomas Matthew Ray during the years 1856-9. At this time workmen employed by the Corporation of Dublin were engaged in sewer-laying in Nicholas Street, Francis Street, Christchurch Place – formerly Skinners Row – and neighbouring streets and Thomas Ray not alone recorded the discoveries of bone combs, bronze pins, horse shoes and other finds but also included sketches of the different strata revealed in the street cuttings and noted the depths at which various antiquities and other features occurred. Ray's diary and a collection of finds which he had acquired were later presented to the Royal Irish Academy and are now preserved in the National Museum of Ireland. The Ray Collection, as it is called, and other groups of objects presented by the Corporation of Dublin and by various individuals during the late nineteenth and early twentieth centuries are of particular significance because they demonstrate that finds of the Viking and medieval period occurred in almost all the areas within the bounds of the old town walls. Many of the older parts of Dublin have not been redeveloped in modern times and in consequence they retain, in a relatively undisturbed state, much of the debris which accumulated there in the course of the past thousand years. In common with other towns of medieval origin where climatic conditions favourable to the preservation of organic materials exist, the accumulation of refuse matter in this fashion is notable but it is to be explained by reason of the fact that in medieval times the present-day system of collection and disposal of domestic and industrial refuse was largely unknown. In short, it may be taken for granted that a great deal more came into the average medieval town in the shape of food, fodder, building stuffs and the raw materials for the many craftsmen living

View of part of High Street excavation with the Synod Hall of Christ Church Cathedral in the background.

Wooden pathway, c. 1 metre wide, and of late eleventh-century date. High Street.

there than ever left it in the form of waste products. For archaeologists, social historians and other research workers engaged in enquiry into the past, systematic investigation of accumulated deposits of this type — by way of archaeological excavation — is capable of adding a fund of information on what may well be otherwise largely undocumented aspects of human activity.

Until 1962 no excavation of this type had been undertaken in Dublin city with the exception of a small area which had been investigated by the National Monuments Branch of the Office of Public Works within the precincts of Dublin Castle. Proposed redevelopment in the neighbourhood of High Street - the principal street in the medieval period - afforded the National Museum an opportunity of excavation in this area and, with the co-operation of the Corporation of Dublin who owned the properties, investigation was carried out, for two six-month seasons in 1962 and 1963, on a plot of ground bordered by High Street, Nicholas Street and Back Lane.

In the preliminary stages of the work, it was noted that the foundations dug for the construction of cellars of houses of eighteenth-century date which bordered these streets had disturbed the ground to an average depth of eight feet below the present street level. Further excavation revealed, however, that there still remained a six-foot thick stratum of occupation debris which had accumulated in the course of centuries over the original ground surface. This dark-coloured stratum which was of a soft bog-like consistency had been referred to by

Thomas Ray, by Charles Haliday and by earlier writers such as Walter Harris[2] and by Richard Stanihurst.[3] These authors were of the opinion that Dublin was built on marshy or boggy soil but as a result of the 1962-3 excavations it is clear that Haliday and others had inadvertently misinterpreted the evidence and it was established that the boggy soil was, in fact, merely the consolidated organic refuse of the early centuries of occupation in the town. The Museum investigations proved also that the first settlers had built their houses on the solid foundations of the underlying boulder clay in Viking times.

Systematic excavation of the six-foot thick stratum resulted in the recovery of a considerable amount of objects and structures ranging in date from the early fourteenth back to the tenth century.

Many of the finds from the earlier levels are of particular interest since they are identical with material from Viking-period towns and trading posts in Norway, Sweden and northern Germany. The finds include a gilt bronze disc brooch decorated in a tenth-century Norse style, the Borre-Jelling style, of which some twenty examples are known in Scandinavia. Other undoubted Norse objects include a number of iron spearheads, an ingot mould made of soapstone which also has a matrix for casting Thor's hammer symbols — small 'good luck' charms normally worn by the Scandinavians in that period — amber beads and pendants, fragments of weighing scales and other miscellaneous items of distinctively Norse type.

Apart from the discovery of objects showing direct contact with Scandinavia, the excavations also revealed evidence of the many different trades and crafts practised by the townspeople. Large numbers of deer antler fragments, bone plates – some blank and some with the teeth sawn – as well as many examples of single-sided bone combs were evidence of the presence of a comb-maker's workshop, and the presence of shoe-makers was attested by a large quantity of scrap leather and a number of shoes. A weaver, too, seems to have worked on the site, for among the more interesting of the finds was a small but highly decorated wooden sword used to beat the weft threads into the warp.

Remains of houses and workshops were also found. The walls of these structures consisted usually of two spaced rows of undressed upright posts in the round which had horizontal layers of rods or wattles, generally of hazel, ash and elm, woven between them. Fairly complete ground plans of two houses were recovered and they suggest that the buildings were single storey structures measuring, on average, 25 feet long and 15 feet wide; a stone-edged hearth was found at the approximate centre of the floor in each house.

At High Street part of the site was occupied in the late twelfth and early thirteenth centuries by leather workers whose clippings and waste pieces formed a deposit over four feet thick in one particular area. Incorporated in this material there were discarded articles of leather indicative of the skills of the craftsmen in that period. These articles included many shoes, including examples of children's boots and shoes. Examination of the leather scrap suggests that this enormous mass resulted not from the labours of a single cobbler but of a community working in the same area over a long period of time. Conspicuous among the leather fragments recovered were a large number of soles, worn, damaged or holed, which suggest that at that time it was not the practice to repair worn soles. It would appear, however, that the uppers, when cut

Above: A storage pit lined with post and wattle. High Street excavation, 1962-3.
Below: Timber-lined pit of thirteenth century — one of several uncovered in the Wood Quay/Winetavern Street excavations.

away from the worn soles, were re-used to make 'new' footwear, usually of a smaller size than the originals. Cattle hides were the source of most of the leather but a number of articles made from goat skin were also present. Many leather knife sheaths were also incorporated in this deposit. Most of these sheaths are decorated with patterns of interlaced and geometrical ornament and one example bears representations of birds with floreated tails.

The occurrence in an adjoining area of the site of considerable numbers of objects made of bone and antler, together with a large amount of waste or rejected items, indicates that craftsmen working in these materials were near neighbours of the leather workers. The discovery of over a hundred examples of single-sided combs, many of them fragmentary and some in various stages of manufacture, indicates the presence of comb makers. The raw material used in the making of the majority of the combs was the antlers of red deer and, although a large quantity of worked and unworked antler was found, very few deer bones were present among the animal food bones which occurred in quantity on the site. It is evident from the presence of natural ruptures on the majority of antler burrs recovered that shed antlers were the main source of supply, and in all likelihood there were persons living in the neighbouring countryside frequented by the deer who took advantage of this situation by collecting the shed antlers in late spring and bringing them to the town for sale to the comb makers.

Some of the objects recovered from early thirteenth-century levels at High Street have associations with persons known from historical records. One example is a lead *bolla* which was originally attached to a Letter Apostolic issued by Pope Innocent III (1198-1216). As is usual on seals of this type, the *bolla* bears on one face a representation of Saints Peter and Paul and on the other the name of the reigning Pope. It is recorded that at least ninety letters were sent to Ireland by Pope Innocent III, many of them relating to the archbishopric of Dublin and Dublin churches. Another object with personal associations is a lead seal matrix which belonged to a certain Adam Burestone. It bears his name and the figure of a centaur in bas-relief. The owner was probably a Norman knight, since the name Burestone occurs in documents of this period in the west of England, a district closely connected with the Anglo-Norman invasion of Ireland. An item which had travelled far is a small pilgrim's badge which is made of pewter. It has a loop at each of its four corners, through which it was sewn to the pilgrim's clothing. It bears the figures of Saints Peter and Paul, the latter holding his emblem, a sword, the former a large key with highly decorative wards. In 1199 Pope Innocent III gave the Canons of Saint Peter's in Rome the sole right of casting badges of this particular type. They were acquired by pilgrims in Rome and worn by them as proofs and as souvenirs of their pilgrimage. It is most probable that the badge in question was brought from Rome by some pilgrim from Ireland who undertook the long hazardous journey there and back in the beginning of the thirteenth century. If he was a Dubliner and a layman he was not the first such adventurous townsman to do so, for the various Irish annals record the departure to Rome between 1028 and 1064 of a series of royal pilgrims, including Sitric, the Norse king of Dublin, and his successor Olaf. It is, however, also worth remembering that Innocent III, whose name appears on the *bolla,* was the Pope who convened the Fourth Lateran Council in 1215 at which were present seventy-one archbishops, four hundred and twelve bishops, eight hundred abbots and innumerable representatives of princes and towns from all over Christendom. It is possible, therefore, that the badge was brought back by someone who travelled officially from Dublin to Rome on that occasion.

Another discovery which has an association with pilgrimages is a small bronze flask or *ampulla* used by pilgrims to carry holy water or consecrated oils obtainable at places of pilgrimage. The flask bears inscriptions in relief of its dedication to the Virgin Mary and Saint Wulfstan. Saint Wulfstan was made bishop of Worcester in 1062 and after his death in 1095 the reputation of sanctity for which he had been noted during his lifetime was enhanced by the occurrence of miracles at his tomb. In 1202 a panel of prelates was appointed to verify the authenticity of Wulfstan's miracles and this commission included John Comyn, archbishop of Dublin. Wulfstan was canonised in 1203 and, although Worcester continued as an important centre of pilgrimage in the middle ages, the *ampulla* from High Street is the only pilgrim souvenir of Worcester which is known to have survived.

The presence of a 'school' of artists and metalworkers in Dublin in the twelfth and eleventh centuries is indicated by the discovery of workshop hearths and numerous examples of carved bone 'trial pieces' — animal ribs and long bones bearing panels of geometric motifs and animal interlacements. The carvings range from preliminary sketches to finished designs executed in full relief and include examples which were apparently rejected because of errors in layout or faulty cutting. The finished designs are considered to have served as patterns for casting in metal the decorative panels used in the contemporary metalwork, of which many examples have survived in the form of croziers and reliquaries. One of the more interesting examples is that bearing motifs in an Irish-Scandinavian style. The main composition, that of two animals each forming a loop and semi-interlaced, is a close parallel to that which is present on one of the panels on the Shrine of the Cathach of Columcille — a shrine made between 1062 and 1098, possibly at Kells in Co. Meath, and now preserved in the National Museum of Ireland.

At Winetavern Street it was found that the upper reaches of the sloping ground between Christ Church Cathedral and the Liffey had been densely inhabited from some time in the tenth century onwards. The remains of this occupation consisted of a layer, 19 feet thick in places, composed of the accumulated refuse of centuries. As at High Street, the later medieval strata had been considerably disturbed as a result of subsequent building operations but stratified material ranging in date from the thirteenth to the tenth centuries was recovered. A number of pits datable to the thirteenth century were found to contain a wide range of discarded materials, including leather shoes and decorated leather knife-sheaths, fragments of cloth, an iron gimlet with a lathe-turned wooden handle and numerous fragments of glazed and unglazed pottery. Many vessels have been reconstructed from these sherds and a number of them have been identified as of French type; they were, presumably, exported together with shipments of wine from the Bordeaux region.

Many of the refuse pits of the thirteenth century and earlier periods have proved of considerable interest in so far as an examination of the refuse which they contained has thrown a flood of new light upon the food, agriculture and animal husbandry of the period. From the seeds and plant fragments preserved

Top: Inscribed double-sided wooden comb from Christchurch Place excavations.

Above left: Decorated leather sheaths of early thirteenth century. One bears designs of two birds with floreated tails.

Above right: A seal matrix bearing the words *Sigillum AD BURESTONE*. It bears the figure of a centaur with a bow and arrow.

in the fill of the pits, it has been possible to compile a long list of species which were utilised by the inhabitants of the town for food and for other purposes. A large number of different kinds of fruits were eaten by the inhabitants: strawberries, apples, cherries, plums, sloes, blackberries, rowan berries, frochans and hazel nuts. In medieval documents relating to Dublin figs are mentioned among the articles which were subject to toll, and the discovery of fig seeds in thirteenth-century pits in Winetavern Street and in High Street proves that these luxuries were, in fact, imported. A matter of some surprise is the fact that the seeds of goosefoot *(Chenopodium)* and three species of *Polygonum* (knotgrass, black bindweed and pale persicaria) were, apparently, extensively used as food. Although now regarded as weeds, the seeds of these plants were widely used as food in Neolithic times. These seeds may, of course, have been used only by the more needy citizens as the examination of material from various pits showed that oats, barley and wheat formed part of the diet.

In thirteenth- twelfth- and eleventh- century levels at Winetavern Street the discovery of many wooden bowls, platters and barrel staves, some in an unfinished state, suggests that woodturners and coopers were settled in this part of the town. Here, too, were found two wooden planks, each bearing an incised sketch of a ship, and two small wooden models of ships.

Although well over two hundred examples of bone combs were recovered at Winetavern Street, the site produced no evidence that comb making was carried on there although at High Street abundant evidence of this craft was discovered.

Selection of leather scraps from cobbler's workshop, uncovered in the course of the High Street excavation.

Jawbone of pig — later
used for 'trial piece' purposes.
Winetavern Street, Dublin.

The combs closely resemble modern combs in shape but the teeth were sawn from a number of plaques of deer antler which were held rigidly in place between two long strips which formed the back of the comb. To protect the teeth, comb cases, also made of antler, were sometimes used and a few complete examples and fragments of many others were discovered.

The finds of individual objects made in the course of excavation were extremely numerous and they throw considerable light on the life and activities of the inhabitants. Their domestic vessels were made of wood and pottery. Those of the former material included circular lathe-turned bowls and large rectangular dishes, each hollowed out of a single piece of wood. Cracks which had appeared in some of them had been repaired with metal stitches to give them another lease of useful life. They also used baskets skilfully made with thin slats of oak for the warp and strips of willow as weft. There is, in addition, a large body of artifacts of a miscellaneous nature which illustrate many other aspects of the contemporary way of life. These include iron locks and keys for doors and chests; spindles and their whorls used in spinning thread; bone gaming pieces; iron knives; fish hooks; and a considerable number of textile fragments, including extraordinary delicate pieces of netting which were, probably, used as hair nets.

Many of the finds from the earlier phases of occupation (tenth to eleventh centuries) have a strong Viking complexion. These include rotary grindstones of a typically Scandinavian type, fragments of soapstone vessels and a small openwork quadrangular bronze brooch, close parallels to which have been found in a ship burial near Bergen in Norway, in a Viking grave in Birka near Stockholm and in the Norse town of Hedeby in Schleswig, north-Germany. Other objects betraying Scandinavian connexions include amber beads, stone moulds for casting silver ingots, ring-headed bronze pins and a series of bone pins with heads carved into animal figurines.

Because of the excellent state of preservation of the material uncovered in these excavations a considerable amount of information can be gleaned not alone from the objects but also from the wooden structures, the refuse pits, pathways and from the soil itself. After its founding in the ninth century, Dublin soon became an important trading and commercial centre and the results of the excavations whilst indicating the importance of certain areas of the town as centres of trades and crafts also provide evidence of contact with other lands, notably Scandinavia, England and France.

CHAPTER 7

HOWARD CLARKE

The Historian and Wood Quay

Historians are normally thought of as people who use written documents to build up a picture of human societies as they existed in the past. Of many historians this is still true, but for others times have changed. For historians of early periods and of material culture, archaeology has in recent decades come to create opportunities for the reinterpretation of old problems and for the increase of our knowledge of the historical past. While documents offer chronological precision, archaeology provides tangible contact with past societies. In the most favourable circumstances the two types of evidence are complementary. The fewer the documents that survive, the greater is the potential of archaeology, reaching back ultimately into 'prehistory'. The divide between prehistory and history is now less sharp than it once appeared: students of the early Middle Ages are becoming conscious of the 'prehistoric' character of this 'historical' period. The reason for this change is that archaeological and documentary techniques have been applied to medieval Europe, particularly since the Second World War, to the intellectual enrichment of both archaeologists and historians.

In the light of the recent controversy focused on medieval Dublin, it is necessary to establish a premise — one that might at first sight seem trite. The premise is that for us to acquire a deeper knowledge of the history of medieval Dublin, irrespective of the ethnic content of that history and of the ethnic background of modern scholars, is a laudable and useful goal. Perhaps not many people with any pretensions to be 'cultured', in the general sense of that word, will object explicitly to this premise. But in certain quarters there is, apparently, an attitude of mind that attaches inferiority or even irrelevance to non-Gaelic aspects of the history of this island. The Vikings are a case in point. The traditional schoolbook view of these Scandinavians as barbaric, ferocious and pagan warriors has been modified considerably by scholars working in these islands and on the Continent. The change of emphasis is twofold: that the Irish themselves were responsible for many attacks on churches, and that the Scandinavian contribution to the development of towns and trade provided a vital stimulus to the economy of medieval Europe.[1]

It is a striking fact that less original work has been done on the history of medieval Dublin since 1921 than before that year. It is a striking fact that no comprehensive and original history of the medieval town has been published. So

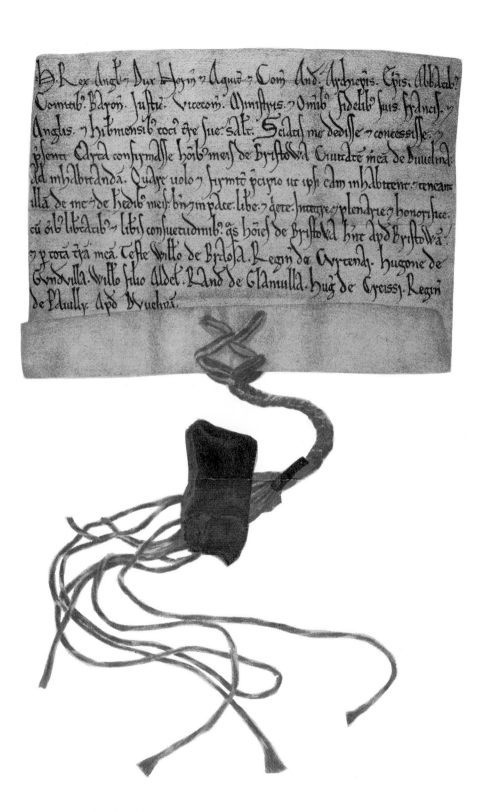

Charter of Henry II, granting Dublin to the men of Bristol, 1171-2.

The Old Tower of Michael of Pole. Dublin.

This Tower is ill Shaped *and this defect Seems to be own to the builder and not to the scurry of Time*

The round tower of the early Irish monastery dedicated to St Michael le Pole as drawn by G. Beranger in the early eighteenth century. It was situated near Ship Street.

long was the interval between the construction of the first permanent Scandinavian settlement in A.D. 841 and the departure of the British in 1921 that very little of Dublin's history is purely Gaelic or Irish. But ethnocentric history is generally bad history. Admirable though it may be as a collection of documentary allusions, the late George Little's work on early medieval Dublin conjures up an absurd picture of a vast Gaelic city in pre-Viking times.[2] Only recently have we begun to face up to the fundamental problems presented by medieval Dublin, such as the significance of the place-names *Áth Cliath* and *Dubhlinn*.[3] To further this process we must cast aside our ethnic blinkers and regard ourselves as part of a broader, and intellectually richer, community of nations.

The bulk of the evidence for the history of medieval Dublin is archaeological and documentary. There are many differences between these two types of evidence; here I should like to draw one basic distinction. When a historian makes use of unprinted documents, he or she returns them afterwards to the custody of the archivist who has charge of them. In other words, when handled with care and preserved in vaults, our documentary heritage is neither diminished nor transformed in normal circumstances. This is why the calculated destruction of a high proportion of the nation's archives in 1922 was a peculiarly objectionable and shameful deed.[4] The irreparable damage that was done by those who were responsible is now appreciated by historians, if not by the public at large. Archaeological material, on the other hand, is *always* vulnerable. While still buried in the ground it suffers from the normal processes of decay and is prone to disturbance or removal in the course of building operations and the provision of underground services. Once artifacts and features have been taken out of their stratigraphical context, there are no means of replacing them. Great responsibility, therefore, rests with developers, landowners and planners, as well as with local and national authorities. The amount of archaeological material in Dublin is finite and is concentrated in a small part of the modern city. Every act of deliberate destruction diminishes the archaeological record and is as irresponsible as the deliberate burning of ancient documents. The consequences of both are irreversible.

Great responsibility rests also with archaeologists. This is why they take elaborate measures to record the layers in which everything is found, in order that chronological and typological sequences may be established. Even if the spoil-heap is retained for inspection, the bulk removal of archaeological material by machinery is essentially destructive, for it is the stratigraphy that is destroyed unrecorded. Of course, archaeological excavation itself removes artifacts and features from their stratigraphical context, but not before the site has been described in minute detail with the aid of drawings and photographs. In addition to small finds, *knowledge* of the site is preserved. Archaeology, then, amounts not to crude destruction, but to the controlled recovery of information. This information has to be analysed and published in full before it can be said that the archaeological process is complete. Full publication of the data makes it possible to reinterpret a site in the future, in the light of new knowledge and new questions. One type of knowledge of interest to historians is sometimes overlooked, namely, quantitative data. The claim that the Dublin excavations are yielding more of the same kind of evidence falls down on two grounds. First, historians are concerned not simply with examples of artifacts from the past; they are concerned equally with how many such artifacts were produced. Economic history thrives on classifiable and quantifiable data, whereas individual finds, no matter how exquisite or valuable, are of limited use. Secondly, the streets of medieval European towns were commonly allocated to different occupation groups, hence many of the characteristic street-names in Dublin, such as Cooks' Street, Skinners' Row and Taverners' Street. Precisely because of this phenomenon, certain crafts are well represented in what has so far been recovered and others hardly at all. This is particularly true of those industries which needed a constant supply of water and which were normally located on the banks of rivers and streams.

The intimate association of archaeology with history may be illustrated by reference to a map of medieval Dublin published by the Ordnance Survey.[5] One of the most important features of this map is the broken line indicating the zone of archaeological potential within the modern city. This zone comprises not only the defended enclosure of the Anglo-Norman town, but also districts outside the walls and north of the River Liffey. Outside the later walls lie sites of Gaelic and Scandinavian interest, including the probable monastic complex referred to in early documents as *Dubhlinn*. Public awareness of medieval Dublin needs to be extended well beyond the visible remains of the stone wall: along Thomas Street, around St Patrick's Cathedral and Aungier Street, and to what medieval Dubliners knew as Oxmantown. The basis for delimiting this archaeological zone is documentary: the historical materials that have survived the hazards of time. These sources suggest a combination of possibilities and probabilities; only archaeological excavation can confirm or confound the efforts of a historian in this direction. But in any evaluation of the archaeological potential of medieval Dublin, it is obvious that historians have a part to play. The institutional infrastructure of Irish archaeology should make provision for the results of documentary analysis to be taken into account.

The Wood Quay archaeological site occupied part of the defended enclosure or, more exactly, it contained parts of a whole succession of defended enclosures. One of the completely unsolved questions about medieval Dublin is the location of the Viking seafort *(longphort)* first constructed in 841.[6] Most writers have assumed that this military base was established somewhere near the later castle, but there is no conclusive evidence, in print, to substantiate this assumption. An alternative suggestion is that the *longphort* was sited at Kilmainham or Islandbridge, near the great ninth-century cemetery.[7] Only the most careful application of archaeological method will provide an answer to this problem: even if artifacts such as coins were to survive the process of bulk removal of archaeological layers by machinery, their crucial dating evidence would be lost. The inner of the two earthen banks found in the south-eastern portion of the Wood Quay site has been dated to *c.* 950,[8] but the curving line of Fishamble Street may itself be a reflection of still earlier defences higher up the slope. Wherever this seafort was located, it had a chequered history. The annalist implies that property was destroyed in 851 when Danish Vikings plundered the Norse settlement.[9] Eventually, in 902, all the Scandinavians were expelled from Dublin by the men of Brega and of Leinster.[10] The exile lasted until 917.

The earliest features to which dates have been assigned by archaeologists working on the site belong to the period when the Scandinavians were re-establishing themselves at Dublin. As might be expected, the Norse settlement was refortified in 917,[11] perhaps by means of earthen banks reinforced by timber, of the kind already discovered. In 936 Scandinavian Dublin was burned by the forces of the Uí Néill king, Donnchad Donn, apparently as a reprisal for a raid on Clonmacnoise.[12] A similar pattern of events occurred three years later: the Dublin Norse plundered Old Kilcullen and were besieged by an army led by the same king and his ally, Muirchertach mac Néill, the king of Ailech. According to the *Annals of the Four Masters* the Scandinavians were again expelled 'with the help of God and St MacTáil'.[13] The revived Norsemen under new leadership slew King Lorcán of Leinster in 943, when he was caught in the act of plundering the settlement.[14] In the following year his death brought forth vengeance on a massive scale. Having secured the assistance of the new high-king, Congalach Cnogba mac Máel Mithig, the leaders of Leinster conducted a successful raid on Norse Dublin. The more elaborate version given in the *Annals of the Four Masters* suggests that houses and ships were burned, warriors were killed in large numbers, and women, children and dependants were carried off into

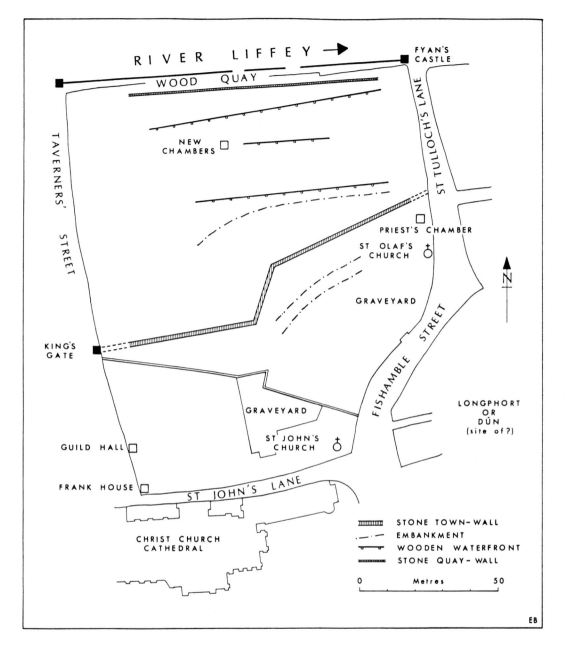

Outline map of the Wood Quay site and its immediate surroundings.

slavery.[15] The high-king raided Dublin again in 947, but nine years later was himself ambushed and killed by the Norsemen, now allied to the men of Leinster.[16] After a three-day siege, Dublin was plundered in 980 by the great army raised by a more famous high-king, Máel Sechnaill mac Domnaill, and again in 995.[17] Three years after this Máel Sechnaill and Brian Bóruma launched a joint attack on Dublin and seized hostages and treasure.[18] Following on from their decisive victory over the Norse and their Leinster allies at the battle of Glenn Máma in 999, the two kings are said to have occupied Dublin for a week, burning

Dublin's oldest surviving building: the crypt of Christ Church, constructed at the end of the twelfth century.

the fortress, or *dún,* and taking away gold, silver and prisoners.[19] In the year after the battle of Clontarf, Máel Sechnaill again burned the fortress and all the houses outside it.[20]

Thus the annalists recorded a whole series of attacks on Dublin between 936 and 1015. This chronology, built up from written documents, needs to be related to the defensive features found at Wood Quay. It may happen that, in future excavations on other sites in the Lord Edward Street area, parts of the same defensive arrangements will be discovered, but there is no guarantee that the evidence has not already been destroyed and, in any case, further opportunities to excavate may not materialise for many years. We have to make maximum use of what is accessible at the moment: future generations will not condone the destruction of evidence that may prove to have been unique. This particular period of Dublin's history is of special importance, for during these years the Norse settlement evolved from a seafort dominated by military considerations and by the slave trade into a place that was recognisably a town.[21] When in 989 Máel Sechnaill mac Domnaill captured Dublin after a twenty-day siege, he imposed a tax of one ounce of gold on each messuage or 'garth' *(garrdha),* which suggests that uniform building plots may already have been laid out.[22] And despite the vicissitudes of political fortune, the town continued to develop and prosper. Part of what appears to have been a westward extension from the original nucleus occupied the south-western quarter of the Wood Quay site. The reference in 1015 to the burning of all the houses outside the *dún* seems to imply that part of the settlement was as yet unenclosed, or at least was less well defended.[23] It is just possible that the conversion of the Dublin Norsemen to Christianity, together with the construction of the first Christ Church Cathedral as their principal church *c.* 1030, had some connection with the enlargement of the defended area. One vital point that needed to be established in the recent excavations was the precise direction in which the earthen banks were heading before they disappeared beneath inaccessible ground. The great achievement of Hiberno-Norse Dublin in the eleventh century was the stone wall that, until 1980, zigzagged so dramatically across the Wood Quay site. If the date *c.* 1100 that has been proposed by archaeologists is correct, this would make Dublin one of the earliest non-Roman towns in Europe to have provided itself with such a means of defence, even though this wall may have lacked the towers characteristic of later medieval town defences. The wall was a tribute to Dublin's prosperity, for stone defences were always expensive to build in the Middle Ages. That Irish kings and high-kings vied with one another for political control of the Hiberno-Norse town is hardly surprising.

At an unknown date the adoption of Christianity by the Norse inhabitants resulted in the construction of another church, St Olaf's. Óláfr Haraldsson, the king of Norway from 1015 to 1030, played an important part in the conversion of that country and, within a year of his death in battle, he was being venerated as a martyr. The church dedicated to him in Dublin may have been founded at about the same time as the cathedral and was in those days situated down by the riverside. That some remains of this church would be uncovered in the recent excavations was expected by many people. It seems to have been forgotten that, forty years ago, traces of St Olaf's were indeed discovered by employees of Dublin Corporation, who were preparing the ground for a petrol pump. Wooden coffins and a quantity of bones were found beneath the remains of a flagged floor supported by brick arches.[24] Either the floor of this church was renewed in the fifteenth or the first half of the sixteenth century, or the brick arches in question were of later date. A priest's chamber stood immediately north of the church and survived into the eighteenth century.[25] Some time before the Anglo-Normans captured Dublin, St John's Church was founded in the angle between Fishamble Street and John's Lane. Though the medieval building has long since been demolished, much of its graveyard still exists and may be capable of yielding important archaeological data if properly conserved. In 1170, according to the *Annals of the Four Masters,* the Dublin Norse were slaughtered in the middle of their own stronghold by the forces of Diarmait Mac Murchada and his Anglo-Norman allies.[26] Thus began a new phase in the history of Dublin.

After 1170 the focus of attention on the Wood Quay site shifts north of the Hiberno-Norse wall to the River Liffey. Here the true potential of large-scale archaeological excavation has been demonstrated, with the physical and intellectual revelation of a whole succession of thirteenth-century waterfronts, culminating *c.* 1300 in the construction of a stone quay-wall at Wood Quay.[27] At least two qualifications need to be made from a historian's point of view. First, the authorities at the National Museum of Ireland began by regarding the area outside the late eleventh-century stone wall as expendable. Ethnocentric archaeology is as deplorable as ethnocentric history: fortunately public opinion in Dublin was more enlightened.[28] Secondly, the fact that drainage channels, refuse pits, big pieces of timber, and other features were still in position for the public to view in the summer of 1977 means that further examination and recording of many parts of the site remained to be done. Only when 'natural' – not necessarily bedrock – has been reached over an entire site can the physical process of excavation be pronounced completed. Archaeological features that are not designated for preservation *in situ* should be fully excavated and removed, for crucial dating evidence may otherwise be destroyed. A country that has already lost the bulk of its public records cannot afford to throw away historical material.

With the richer documentation of the Anglo-Norman period, some written evidence becomes available for particular buildings on the Wood Quay site. Even so, for most buildings there is no documentation and our sole resource is archaeology. One documented structure is the old Guild Hall, which stood at the upper end of Winetavern Street adjacent to a messuage belonging to Vincent Taverner. This building was made partly of stone, but by 1311 all except its two cellars had been demolished.[29] On the corner of Winetavern Street and John's Lane may have stood the Frank (free) House, so called because it was held by the Knights Hospitaller and was exempt from local taxation.[30] According to an item in the Chain Book of the city of Dublin, a lane provided a short-cut from the King's Gate in Winetavern Street to Fishamble Street just north of St John's Church.[31] This lane passed along the northern perimeter of St John's graveyard and still did so in the middle of the eighteenth century.[32] An opportunity to excavate a medieval street comes relatively rarely; cross-sections through the successive layers of road-surfacing materials can be valuable for dating purposes. A late medieval building known as New Chambers was sited somewhere near Wood Quay, but its remains may have been removed in the course of cellar construction or machine excavation.[33] Part of the late medieval defences consisted of a four-storey tower situated at the north-eastern corner of the Wood Quay site. Early in 1456 it was leased to a merchant named John Marcus for a term of thirty years at an annual rent of 6d.[34] In the sixteenth century this tower became known as Fyan's Castle, from a lessee of that name. When in 1585 Fyan's Castle was surveyed under the direction of Sir John Perrot, it was found to measure 38 feet by 20 feet, with walls 4 feet thick.[35] Nearly four centuries later, in 1975, its substantial foundations were severely damaged by machinery working under the direction of Dublin Corporation.

The Wood Quay site, extending as it did from near the crest of the ridge on which Dublin was built to the River Liffey, was a microcosm of the medieval town. Its archaeological record as a habitation site is known to reach back in time as far as the middle of the tenth century. One of the many historical mysteries relating to Dublin is linked with the old name for the lower part of Fishamble Street, St Tulloch's Lane. This is derived from an alternative name for St Olaf's Church, while Tulloch, or Tullock, has been thought to be a corruption of the Irish name, *Duilech*. The strongest associations of St Duilech, who flourished *c*. 600, are with Balgriffin, [36] and a different explanation is to be found in London, where Óláfr became Tooley.[37] Some time after the coming of the Anglo-Normans to Ireland, this Norse name was similarly corrupted in at least three towns – Dublin, London and Wexford[38] – for reasons that necessarily remain obscure. Amid so much documentary obscurity, therefore, what is required is that urban archaeology in Dublin should be placed on a sound and regular footing; otherwise the potential that has already been demonstrated will be lost beyond recovery. This potential relates not only to medieval Dublin, but also to post-medieval Dublin: the archaeology of the sixteenth and seventeenth centuries is as valid as that of the tenth and eleventh centuries. Broad-mindedness rather than narrow-mindedness, a long-term view rather than a short-term view, imaginative forethought rather than entrenched attitudes — these positive qualities alone will ensure that the rest of medieval Dublin is left with a history that can be written. The alternative here will be for historians to write the history of the guilty men whose ambition, greed, ineptitude or shortsightedness destroyed these archaeological remains, along with the historical knowledge they represent. In human affairs the judgement of history is final.

CHAPTER 8

ANNGRET SIMMS

A Key Place for Dublin Past and Present

As a historical geographer my happiest memory of Wood Quay is of the time of the guided tours during the summer of 1977, when thousands of people walked on the medieval stone wall and glimpsed for the first time the physical origins of their town through the assemblage of archaeological features left on the site. It was easy for them to understand that Dublin began as a settlement along the waterfront. My worst memory of the site is of October 1980, when I walked with some students up Fishamble Street and found that the viewing platform had not been shifted, although the archaeological excavations had moved up the street some time previously; the medieval stone wall was being dismantled by a group of building workers, and bulldozers were moving on ground that, a short time before, had held the fabric of the first streets and houses of Dublin. The anger of the students was intense, probably because they instinctively realised that in a democratic society the preservation or neglect of historical monuments reflects fairly closely the cultural consciousness of that society.

It is in the field of education that the significance of Wood Quay is greatest. The historical geographer is mainly interested in three areas: the significance of the site for the people of Dublin as part of their visible history; the importance of the archaeological excavations as source material for the topography of early medieval Dublin; and the relevance of the Wood Quay excavations to comparative studies of the origin of towns in other parts of Europe.

THE IMPORTANCE OF 'PLACE'

Wood Quay is a key place for the early history of Dublin. In recent years there has been a growing consciousness among social scientists of the importance of the concept of 'place' for those who plan our cities. The 'spaces' that our cities fill become 'places' if they are transformed by meaning. We assign meaning to a place if we identify with it, for example our home. We assign meaning to a town, if we identify with its history as part of our search for roots. Such an attachment to place becomes necessarily a relationship of concern, which is the basis for good citizenship. The opposite of attachment to place is 'placelessness'. It is the result of the weakening of identity of place through modern technocratic decisions which produce uniformity of towns all over the world.

Recently, geographers have rediscovered the importance of the interpretation of places, through the use of original sites, to reveal meaning and relationships rather than simply to communicate factual information. It is precisely this concept that made the guided tours of Wood Quay in the summer of 1977 such an unexpected success. People learned about the origin of their city and greatly enjoyed the experience. This kind of enjoyment goes beyond the private sphere because it helps to deepen our identification with the history of our capital and, in the final analysis, makes us better citizens, conscious of the efforts of our predecessors in building up the town in which we live today. Tragically, these guided tours cannot be repeated because the archaeological monuments no longer exist. The earthen banks have been levelled, the stone wall has been dismantled, the wooden revetments have been pulled out and none of the many excavated Viking houses have been preserved *in situ.*

The Irish people did their best to avoid this irresponsible destruction, but their opinion was ignored by Dublin Corporation and the Government. The damage has been done and is intensely regretted far beyond Ireland. Already in 1975, before the Wood Quay saga had reached the courts, the Irish attitude to preservation was strongly criticised in a major textbook edited by M. W. Barley in 1975, *European Towns: Their Archaeology and History* by the following statement: 'Ireland, Italy and Scotland suffered particularly regrettable losses of the historic fabric of their city-centres due to economic pressure from leading speculators backed up by a state and local bureaucracy'. The loss is all ours!

The new Dublin Corporation Civic Offices on Wood Quay (fig. 1).

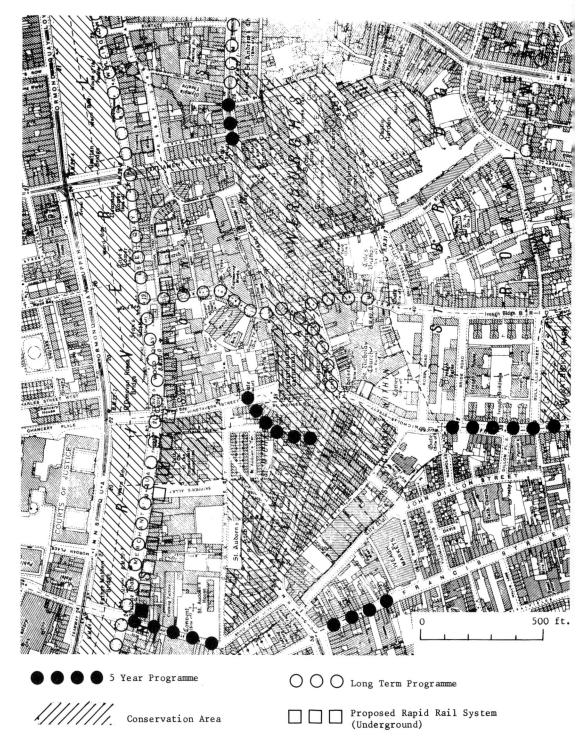

Legend:

●●●● 5 Year Programme

○○○ Long Term Programme

/////// Conservation Area

□□□ Proposed Rapid Rail System (Underground)

Road proposals for Medieval Dublin (fig. 2), (based on the Dublin City Development Plan, Draft Review, 1980).

The loss of a chance to learn at first hand about the origin of the city, the loss of a chance to use the commercial viability of the preservation of the past.

The National Monument in the core of Medieval Dublin should have been preserved as a symbol of the continuity of human purpose in the city. The building of eight-storey office blocks destroys the fabric of the medieval town because it interferes with its scale (Fig. 1). Any straightening and widening of roads in that area eliminates the continuity of a thousand years.

The road programme of Dublin Corporation includes straightening and widening Fishamble Street and Werburgh Street and breaking a new road from High Street to Winetavern Street, all inside the walled town. St Patrick Street, leading up to it, is to suffer the same fate (Fig. 2). These decisions must have originated, *before* Medieval Dublin existed in the mind of the planners. In 1967 the *Advisory Plan and Final Report on Dublin* included a map showing O'Connell Street and Grafton Street as the heart of Dublin, leaving a blank for the walled medieval town. In the Dublin City Development Plan Draft Review of 1976 *Medieval Dublin* is not recognised at all as a distinct part of the city. Therefore, in a submission to this Plan the Friends of Medieval Dublin asked that Medieval Dublin be given the same status as Georgian Dublin. It is very welcome that the most recent City Development Plan of 1980, should include the following statement:

> In the medieval town it shall be policy to respect, as far as possible, the character of the medieval street pattern, and to include provision for trial borings and excavations before building on the sites listed in List 4.

List 4 contains those sites recorded on the 1978 Ordnance Survey map: *Dublin c. 840 to c. 1540: The Medieval Town in the Modern City.*

This policy statement will become effective, only if it is decided *who* is in fact responsible for the payment of trial borings and rescue excavations. Goodwill alone is no longer sufficient where demands for the preservation of historic heritage and modern economic interests clash.

THE IMPORTANCE OF THE EARLY MEDIEVAL SITE

The destruction of this National Monument is a sign of disregard for the cultural needs of the people. But, thanks to the Wood Quay excavations, we have at least gained in another field: we have increased our *knowledge* about the origins of Ireland's capital city. Let's just look at one particular aspect, namely the way in which the early medieval settlers at Wood Quay used the topography of the site. A comparison of the first topographical map of Dublin, 1610 (Fig. 4) with the contour map (Fig. 3) shows that one of the major characteristics of medieval towns was their adaptability to the natural site. On the contour map the most dominant feature is the long narrow ridge running parallel to the Liffey at a height of approximately fifty feet, as far as the confluence with the River Poddle. The map shows how in the medieval period the Poddle had a free run around the eastern edge of the ridge. It was culverted only in the nineteenth century. The ridge consists of boulder clay and was probably once covered with hazelwood. Steep slopes lead down to the north, east and south. Today the streets in that area have steep gradients, particularly Fishamble Street, Werburgh Street and

Nicholas Street. The ridge, as the map shows so clearly, formed a spur, which was ideal in terms of strategic requirements. No wonder, then, that the Vikings chose this site for their encampment when they came sailing up the Liffey in search of a settlement site in the ninth century.

Another notable physical feature, highlighted in Wood Quay, that influenced the growth of early Dublin was the extent of the Liffey estuary, which was much wider in the medieval period than it is today. Excavations on Wood Quay have uncovered the medieval stone wall and there is evidence from marine deposits that the Liffey skirted this wall at high tide. The wall runs approximately along the thirty-foot contour line. Interestingly, this line coincides more or less with the division between the alluvium and the boulder clay as depicted on the geological drift map.

The earthen banks on Wood Quay which predate the stone wall must be seen in this context of a shallow estuary with the likelihood of floods from the river, as well as attacks from raiders. The brushwood matting found on the ground behind the earthen banks are another indication of the problems of wet-ground near the waterfront encountered by the first settlers. The Viking houses were built slightly uphill on firmer ground aligned along present-day Fishamble Street, which points to a continuity of this street for about a thousand years (Fig. 5).

A difficult question which has not yet been answered is whether the first settlement grew from the waterfront up to the ridge or from the ridge down to the waterfront. Also, the task of relating the plot boundaries excavated from the Viking period to the plot boundaries on Rocque's map of Dublin from 1756, which is the first accurately surveyed map of Dublin, is still ahead of us. At one place in Fishamble Street the archaeologists found that different layers of boundary posts went through three centuries of debris, indicating the continuity of property boundaries from the tenth to the twelfth century inclusive. A comprehensive street-plan of the Hiberno-Norse town is not yet available. It remains to be compiled by the archaeologists who did the actual surveying on the site. But it seems certain that the crest of the hill was the main axis of development and that it predated the building of the first church on the site of Christ Church Cathedral. If the church had constituted an important early nucleus there would have been a concentric street-pattern around it, and there is no indication of this in the Wood Quay excavations (Fig. 6).

Another unforgettable lesson that the visitors to the site learned during the summer of 1977 was that all the land between the Hiberno-Norse stone wall and the present-day course of the Liffey was the result of land reclamation by the Anglo-Normans during their first fifty years in Dublin. They needed greater depth of water along the quays for their cargo-boats, and that is why they undertook this tremendous engineering job. In July 1977 rows of the wooden quaywalls were still standing *in situ* and the whole sequence of extending the town into the valley of the Liffey from the earthen banks (tenth to eleventh century) to the stone wall (eleventh century) to the wooden quay walls (thirteenth century) to the final stone wall along the Liffey (fourteenth century) was very clear to the observer. There are also documentary references to land reclamation under the Anglo-Normans. In a confirmation of the original grant of the City of Dublin, issued in the 1190s, we find the recommendation that the inhabitants should lay out land in individual plots with a dwelling house and outbuildings. Some of these were to be laid out

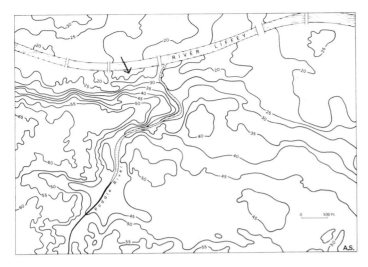

Above: Modern contour map of the medieval part of the city (fig. 3). (The Poddle runs underground today and the course of the Liffey has been artificially straightened.) The arrow indicates the location of Wood Quay.

Below: Speed's map of Dublin, 1610 (fig. 4).

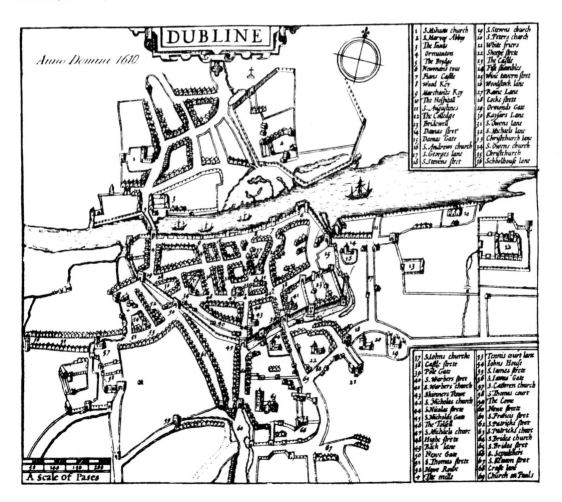

159

Wood Quay excavation site (fig. 5).
1 Christ Church Cathedral;
2 High Street;
3 Fishamble Street;
4 Winetavern Street;
5 Wood Quay, street along the River Liffey;
6 location of the earthen banks, the first fortifications of Dublin from the Viking period (10th and early 11th centuries);
7 town wall built of stone from the Hiberno-Norse period (early 12th century);
8 location of wooden revetments for the reclamation of land along the Liffey by the Anglo-Normans (mainly early 13th century);
9 alignment of the stone wall built in the 14th century;
10 site of excavated wooden houses dated 10th and 11th centuries aligned to the present-day run of Fishamble Street.

over the water, which seems to imply that land was to be reclaimed. Another document, interesting in this context, was issued in 1202 when John, King of England, confirmed Christ Church Holy Trinity in its numerous possessions. The text ends with the following sentence: 'He grants all these with their appurtenances in churches and chapels, in sands and mudbanks.'

THE IMPORTANCE OF EARLY MEDIEVAL DUBLIN FOR EUROPEAN STUDIES

The Viking excavations in Dublin at Wood Quay, and earlier at High Street, have made an important contribution to our knowledge of the early history of towns in Europe outside the area of the Roman Empire. In fact, the Dublin excavations have provided evidence for an early period of town-growth linked with the emergence of coastal trading places from the ninth century onwards, for which archaeological excavations in Scandinavia and the west-Slavic countries have also provided evidence. This early town-growth is based on the emancipation of tradesmen and craftsmen from a rural society in order to satisfy special

Medieval Dublin: growth stages of the walled town - a conjectural reconstruction (fig. 6).
A Viking encampment: pre-urban nucleus
B Viking expansion along High Street: trading centre (town walls from the 12th century)
C Norman expansion by land-reclamation from the Liffey Estuary: fully fledged medieval town (extent of town wall in the 14th century)

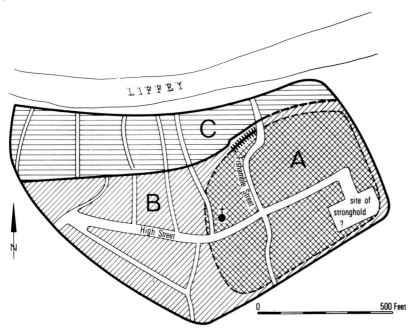

conjectured line of earthen defences   — — — —

area where three parallel earthen banks were excavated   ++++++++++

Christ Church Cathedral (site of the wooden church built in 1030 by King Sitric; present building originated in the Norman period)

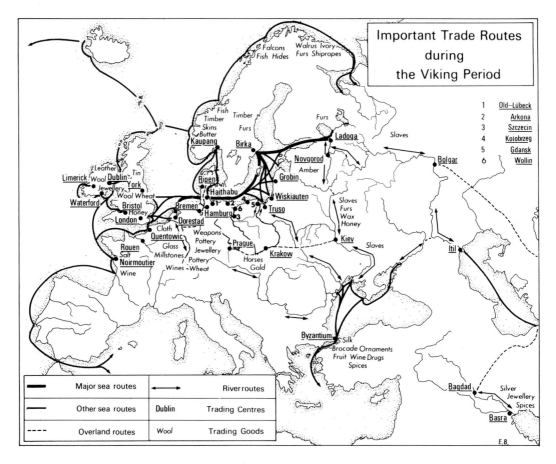

Important trade routes during the Viking period (based on H. Jankuhn), (fig. 7).

consumer needs. This economic and social transformation was the necessary precondition for the formation of towns. Jankuhn (1977) called these early trading places 'simple towns of the old pattern', or 'proto-towns', in contrast to 'towns of the new pattern' which emerged in the twelfth century and were marked by a charter, a municipal legal system and municipal independence. It is due to excavations like those in Dublin that we no longer take our criteria for the definition of towns from constitutional and legal history, but rather look at the economic and social development of the settlement. Viking and Hiberno-Norse Dublin had no charter, but the evidence of settlement density, the existence of workshops and the evidence for long-distance trade certainly point towards a trading centre.

In fact, in the eleventh and early twelfth century Dublin was one of the most important trading towns of Europe, at a time when places like Berlin or Stockholm were mere villages! The characteristic location of these early trading posts of the Viking period was peripheral to countries and entirely sea-orientated (Fig. 7). Most of these trading places, like Dublin, originated as *wiks,* that is to say temporary markets for long-distance traders on their way between the Scandinavian countries and their various trading destinations, exchanging slaves for silver and other luxury goods. From this early function as *wiks* they developed into permanent trading settlements backed up by a class of craftsmen. This is an important point because for a long time the opinion had prevailed that the Vikings had imported towns fully fledged from Scandinavia to their colonies. The fact is that they brought the innovation of long-distance trade and the growth of towns emerged as the product of the Viking period itself. The fabric of the individual trading places was local. This becomes abundantly clear from the post-and-wattle buildings excavated by Pat Wallace at Wood Quay.

Research in recent years has shown that there were quite a number of early west-Slavic trading places along the southern coastline of the Baltic as early as the ninth century. From the tenth century onwards these trading places, whether west-Slavic like Wollin or Germanic like Haithabu, have fortifications consisting of half-circular enclosures of earthen banks topped by palisades. The earthen banks of Viking Dublin at Wood Quay probably belong within this category of fortifications.

By continental standards the early medieval town of Dublin, enclosed by the stone wall, was small, measuring about 12 hectares. The contemporary Belgian trading-post of Dorestadt had 100 hectares of enclosed space. The Swedish trading place of Birka with 12 hectares of enclosed space and Haithabu on the German-Danish border with 24 hectares were closer in size to Dublin. The Slavic stronghold-settlements with their *sub-urbiums* were much smaller, for example Gdansk and Opole, both in Poland, had between 1 and 2 hectares of walled space and Poznan had 5 to 7 hectares.

In a lecture to the Royal Irish Academy in June 1978 Professor Lech Leciejewicz from Warsaw stressed the parallels between the origin of towns in Poland and Ireland. In both countries there were incipient towns or proto-towns founded by a Slav or Hiberno-Norse population respectively. These were succeeded by chartered towns founded by incoming people, German and Norman colonizers respectively. It is this dual ethnic origin which is of particular interest in the Irish context. The early history of Dublin is of great significance generally for the study of urban origins against a background of racial and cultural contact and conflict.

The great importance of Wood Quay goes far beyond the scholarly interest, important though that is. The purely scientific presentation of the excavation results will not be able to convey the degree of understanding resulting from the experience of the site with the archaeological monuments *in situ*. It is the authenticity of a place like Wood Quay which is an irreplaceable asset. Having lived in Central Europe during the Second World War, I know of the sorrow of people who saw their architectural heritage destroyed. To lose an important part of one's heritage by deliberate destruction during peacetime is an added tragedy.

CHAPTER 9

JOHN DE COURCY

Medieval Banks of the Liffey Estuary

On a still autumn day in A.D. 850, the tide being full in, and no flood in the river, the surface of the water in Dublin Bay and in the estuary of the Liffey as far as Kilmainham would have been, to all intents and purposes, a horizontal plane, at a level corresponding to what would today be called + 5.0 m. O.D., or perhaps a little lower. This surface would have covered mud and shingle flats and somewhere through this tideway would have been passing the channel of the river. The same happens today, and the high-tide level remains very much the same as it was then, although the training of the river during the last 1100 years has reduced the tideway for much of its length to a width little greater than that of the channel.

If the limits of the tideway are regarded as the banks of the river and its estuary, it is interesting to speculate just where those banks were during medieval times and how they have changed their position with the development of Dublin. The year 850 is taken as an early medieval date, and as representing a time geologically recent, but before any significant changes had been made to the banks. In such a speculation, one is thinking somewhat surprisingly about some eleven miles of river and estuary banks, measured from Fairview Strand to Merrion Gates by way of Kilmainham. These banks in plan would probably have had, for much of their length, the gentle curves that one sees today in, for instance, the estuary of the Boyne below Drogheda and its outfall to the sea.

Now, one might set out to locate the banks by saying first that they represented very approximately the five-metre contour as it then existed. If one could estimate where that contour ran, one could suggest that that was where the banks were. There are three groups of indicators that have a bearing on the location of this contour. The first is the identification, from trial borings made for modern building investigations, of the surface levels of 'pre-man' ground at various places, and the interpolation from these levels of the five-metre contour as it existed in A.D. 850. The second is the group of historical constructions and sites which might have been presumed to lie on or near the medieval water's edge. The third is the correlation of the contour found from the first two with the present day contours and general lie of the land in areas where man has perhaps made relatively little change to the ground level. Clearly all these groups have inherent weaknesses, which in a fuller study should be stated and ranked, but it seems in order to observe that when compared, they do not in general display

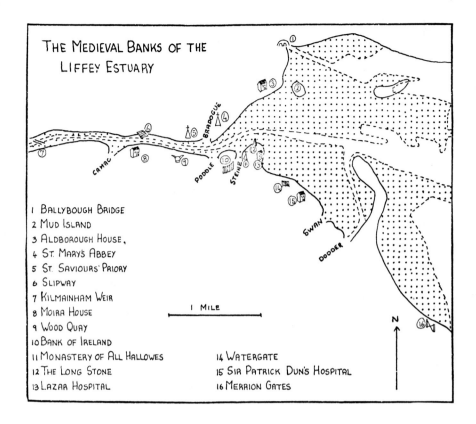

THE MEDIEVAL BANKS OF THE LIFFEY ESTUARY

1 BALLYBOUGH BRIDGE
2 MUD ISLAND
3 ALDBOROUGH HOUSE,
4 ST. MARY'S ABBEY
5 ST. SAVIOURS' PRIORY
6 SLIPWAY
7 KILMAINHAM WEIR
8 MOIRA HOUSE
9 WOOD QUAY
10 BANK OF IRELAND
11 MONASTERY OF ALL HALLOWES   14 WATERGATE
12 THE LONG STONE   15 SIR PATRICK DUN'S HOSPITAL
13 LAZAR HOSPITAL   16 MERRION GATES

incompatible findings, and they do appear to suggest a reasonable location for the medieval banks.

A simple uncritical listing of the indicators in the second group, moving westward along the northern shore, would include Ballybough Bridge, Mud Island - probably in the vicinity of Charleville Avenue - Aldborough house, St Mary's Abbey, the Priory of Saint Saviour, the shingle slipway that cut through the present Ellis Quay until about 150 years ago, and the weir at Kilmainham. Then, moving downstream on the southern shore, one might note Moira House and the puzzling Usher's Island, the north wall and towers of the medieval town, the recently excavated riverside works at Wood Quay, Hoggen Green, the old shore at the Bank of Ireland in College Green, the Monastery of All Hallowes, the Long Stone, Lazars Hospital, the probable existence of watergates on Denzille's Lane, the wrecking of a boat at Sir Patrick Dun's Hospital, Watery Lane as an early name for Lansdowne Road, the kilometre-long spit tipped by Ringsend, and the existence to this day of a substantial area of Sandymount below the five metre level.

Using the first two groups of indicators, the medieval north bank might be seen as commencing close to the present Ballybough Bridge, curving around north of the Charleville Avenue area, then passing south of Aldborough House — which would have been built on the end of the ridge forming the Tolka-Liffey watershed — then perhaps moving in a broad sweep along Sean McDermott Street, passing to the south of the Rotunda Hospital, past Jervis Street Hospital to the

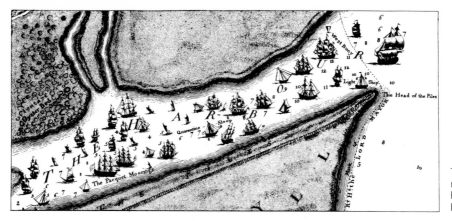

The mouth of the river Liffey from Rocque's map of Dublin, 1757.

south of St Mary's Abbey where it would have been cut by the mouth of the Bradogue. From there it would have followed a line parallel to the existing north quays but possibly 50 metres more or less to the north of them until, having passed along Benburb Street, it entered the 'gorge' formed by the Phoenix Park and the high Camac-Liffey watershed ridge on which the Royal Hospital stands.

The south bank, coming down stream, would first have broken for the Camac and then would have followed a course roughly parallel to the south quays, possibly forming the island known as Usher's Island (which otherwise may have been man-made at a later date), and kept in check by the high ridge of the Poddle-Liffey watershed on which the medieval town was built. East of the Poddle confluence the spread of the medieval estuary would have begun, with the bank passing through the Bank of Ireland in College Green, turning north across the Steine past the northern boundary of Trinity College to form a blunt promontory on or near which the Long Stone and Lazars Hospital stood towards the west end of Townsend Street, then widening again to run through College Park, Lincoln Place, Denzille Lane and Beggarsbush Barracks, and perhaps passing the Swan confluence to meet the Dodder near Lansdowne Road railway station. From there the great Ringsend spit swung out like a giant boomerang, the bank passing around the present Ringsend and returning to run along Tritonville Road, with the spit being possibly not more than about 150 to 200 metres wide in places. Notionally then the coast, for by now it is a definite sea coast, may have lain roughly along the railway line from Serpentine Avenue to Merrion Gates, where we leave it.

These then in a general way could have been the limits of the sheet of water on that autumn day in 850. That there were local irregularities, creeks, influences from tributaries, perhaps rock outcrops, goes without saying. Quite surely also there were changes as the medieval period passed. It is however hard to see these details and changes being identified with any precision, although pieces of the jigsaw will undoubtedly be fitted in from time to time. It is of interest to note that some eight hundred years after the base-date selected, two surveyors, Speed in 1610 and, more significantly in the present context, de Gomme in 1673 plotted the banks as they then found them. These appear to be the earliest formal maps of the area with which we are concerned; and still speaking in a very general way and taking the time interval into account, they can be seen as not in too violent conflict with locations which have been tentatively suggested in this note.

FUTURE
POTENTIAL

CHAPTER 10

THE FRIENDS OF
MEDIEVAL DUBLIN 1984

A Policy for
Medieval Dublin

The events of the Wood Quay saga have shown the widespread interest in the protection and conservation of our archaeological heritage and it is evident that there is a need for planning authorities to prepare development plans which will ensure that the historic cores of Irish towns and cities are properly conserved and preserved. In 1982 a sub-committee of the Friends of Medieval Dublin prepared a Policy for Medieval Dublin which aimed at outlining briefly the problems associated with modern development in the area of medieval Dublin and the possible solutions. It was circulated to members of Dublin Corporation and Dáil Éireann and received a unanimously favourable response. It is included here in the hope that the lessons of Wood Quay will be learned: that Dublin's rich archaeological heritage will be recognised for what it is – unique – and that steps will be taken to ensure that events like the Wood Quay débâcle will not happen again.

A POLICY FOR MEDIEVAL DUBLIN

The Friends of Medieval Dublin was established in 1976 as a study group to increase knowledge about medieval Dublin and to promote public interest in it.

We seek to draw attention to the treasure that is medieval Dublin and to propose a policy by which the redevelopment of the old city centre can go hand in hand with a consistent policy of exploration and conservation of the archaeological wealth of the area.

The value of medieval Dublin for tourism has, as yet, hardly been realised. The medieval town could be a major positive economic asset in the life of the modern city and in the country as a whole. Accurate knowledge and imaginative planning could make this possible. The work should begin *now*. There is danger in delay.

INTRODUCTION

1.1 In June 1978 an area of medieval Dublin of about two acres at Wood Quay was declared by the High Court to be a *national monument;* that is, 'a monument, the preservation of which is a matter of national importance'. The declaration was sought only for that portion (roughly the southern half) of the Civic Offices site at Wood Quay then under immediate threat of destruction and was granted in full. This decision highlighted the importance of medieval Dublin as a whole.

1.2 Shortly after the court decision in 1978 the Ordnance Survey published a map entitled *Dublin c.840–c.1540: the Medieval Town in the Modern City,* prepared for the Friends of Medieval Dublin by Dr H. B. Clarke of University College, Dublin. In this policy the words 'medieval Dublin' refer to the zone of permanent medieval settlement shown on the map by a broken orange line and designated as the 'main zone of archaeological potential'. The line encloses not only the walled town of ca. 18 hectares (44 acres) but also medieval suburbs. A small-scale map showing this area is incorporated here for guideline purposes.

Most of Dublin's early houses were constructed of wood like this example of a late medieval timber-framed house formerly in Castle Street and demolished in the early nineteenth century.

St Michan's church on the north side of the Liffey. Its dedication suggests that there may have been a settlement around it prior to the coming of the Normans.

1.3 Until 1960 virtually nothing was known about the remains of medieval Dublin *below* street level; so little was visible *above* street level that 'medieval Dublin' was barely a recognised concept. Archaeological excavations since 1960 have shown that the site of the medieval town is represented by archaeological deposits between two and ten metres in depth. These deposits contain an invaluable record of Dublin's history from its foundation to the present day. Only a small part (under 2 per cent) of medieval Dublin has been excavated archaeologically since 1960; more has been destroyed without adequate record, and much is sealed off (or already destroyed) beneath permanent buildings and roadways. Nevertheless, well over half of the medieval town area consists of rundown or derelict areas liable to redevelopment in the short or medium term. This situation can either offer a great opportunity for archaeological research or cause widespread archaeological destruction. The outcome will depend on what steps are taken over the next few years, beginning now with a clear policy and positive proposals.

1.4 This archaeological underlay beneath medieval Dublin can be uncovered only by means of scientific excavation. The detailed history that it records can be 'read' only once. We can either read it now, or preserve it to be read later, or destroy it. If we destroy it unread, there will be no other way to recover the information that it now contains.

1.5 The Friends of Medieval Dublin is concerned that under present conditions the remains of medieval Dublin are inadequately protected and are subject to constant damage. Our purpose in issuing this policy is to suggest ways in which this situation can be remedied.

At the heart of these recommendations is the proposition that the Corporation of Dublin, on behalf of its citizens, should put itself at the forefront of the efforts to explore, understand and preserve the remains relating to its own origins.

It is most welcome that the Dublin City Development Plan 1980 contains reference (paragraph 2.5.1) to 'the medieval core with its characteristic street pattern and historic sites' and a proposal that 'in the medieval town it shall be policy to respect, as far as possible, the character of the medieval street pattern and to include provision for trial borings and excavations before building on the sites listed in List 4 [see 3.1 below]. In particular, provision will be made for the preservation of medieval stone structures and, where possible, their incorporation in new buildings' (paragraph 2.5.6). We urge that these proposals should be provided with legal effectiveness.

1.6 There is an urgent need for *special* planning and development controls in the zone of archaeological potential. At the same time such controls should not prevent proper and desirable redevelopment, including housing, which is both essential and long overdue.

Dublin Castle. Excavations here in 1961 showed that it was constructed in the early thirteenth century on top of the remains of Viking houses. Its proposed redevelopment as a European Conference Centre allows opportunity for renewed archaeological excavations.

1.7 This document is concerned with the *medieval core* of Dublin, where the archaeological remains are richest and the potential loss most severe. It is also a matter of concern, however, that the modern city has spread in recent years over a large area and that many formerly autonomous settlements of great antiquity now lie within its boundaries. Such areas as Howth, Finglas, Castleknock, Kilmainham, Tallaght and Newcastle each contain their own small medieval core area, which should be identified and protected from uncontrolled archaeological destruction.

THE PLANNING MATRIX

2.1 The Dublin City Development Plan 1980, which evolved from the statutory review of the 1971 Plan, is the current instrument that determines what kinds of development are permissible in the various areas of the capital city.

2.2 The planning permission system is the mechanism by which any particular development proposal is tested against the general provisions of the plan, and approved or refused accordingly. An Bord Pleanála may reverse, modify or confirm those decisions on application from the developer or a third party.

The important categories of development that are exempt from this careful scrutiny by the Corporation's planning department are those carried out by central government, certain state companies and the local authority itself. This is all the more significant in view of the fact that Dublin Corporation *is a major landowner* of derelict sites in the medieval core area.

2.3 Special protection of the archaeological, architectural, and historical wealth of the city of Dublin should be based firmly on specific provisions in the Development Plan. Only then can the detailed planning permission mechanism be used effectively to safeguard the designated areas and monuments of medieval Dublin.

ARCHAEOLOGY AND THE DEVELOPMENT PLAN

3.1 The Dublin City Development Plan 1980 contains at paragraph 4.2.10 a recognition, for the first time, of the archaeological significance of the medieval core area by the inclusion of a list of 73 sites of archaeological interest (table 4.2.4) [i.e. List 4] under the general heading 'Preservation and Protection of Buildings'. The actual commitment to these sites, however, is minimal, since the plan specifies that the Corporation '*may,* in the event of a planning application being made, require trial borings or excavations to be undertaken prior to commencement of development'.

3.2 The recent Corporation amenity schemes at St Audoen's Park have made an improvement to the area in general, but insufficient attention was paid to the archaeological aspects of the site; proper archaeological supervision of site clearance and mechanical excavation would have led to the recovery of much valuable information, as on any site within the medieval town. In the case of Wood Quay it was the total incompatibility of the architect's design with the archaeological realities of the site that led to the confrontation. Only a complete re-design of the whole project, or an unacceptably long delay in construction to allow for complete archaeological excavation of the site, could have solved the problem.

3.3 The construction of modern tall buildings requires foundations, and sometimes multiple basements, which may necessitate the removal of all 'soft fill' down to bedrock. In medieval Dublin the soft fill contains the archaeological layers, the unrecorded history of early Dublin.

Portion of Dublin's medieval town wall in Cornmarket, off High Street, with the tower of St Audoen's church in the background. It is regrettable that no attempt has been made to highlight this monument in a way befitting its importance.

A historic walking tour, organised by the Friends of Medieval Dublin, outside St Audoen's Gate with the tower blocks of Wood Quay in the background.

How not to develop a medieval street! The proposed motorway plans for Patrick Street showing St Patrick's Cathedral on the right. The broadening of medieval streets to permit heavy through traffic is totally in conflict with the maintenance of a historic core. The alignment of medieval streets as well as their width ought not to be altered.

3.4 Owing to the great depth of deposits, and to the richness of these deposits as archaeological evidence, the proper excavation of an area of any size in medieval Dublin is a slow and expensive business, quite out of proportion to the normal provision of finance for the existing archaeological services in the country.

3.5 The provision of archaeological finance even at the quite exceptional level which prevailed at the height of the Wood Quay operation, that is about £2 million over eight years, would satisfy only a small part of the demand for 'rescue' excavation that could arise if central Dublin were to experience a new property boom.

3.6 It would therefore seem desirable that special incentives should be made available to encourage the right kind of architectural development in the medieval core, which would not interfere with the archaeological layers. These layers can sometimes be sealed off by reinforced concrete rafts and preserved under the new buildings just as they were similarly sealed off and preserved under the old buildings along Fishamble Street that were so recently demolished. This was the method agreed to for a proposed hotel development at High Street.

3.7 It should also be remembered, in view of the difficulties facing the archaeologists of recent times, that funds for excavation alone are not sufficient. They must be accompanied by at least equal provision for post-excavation expenses for conservation, research and, what is of great importance, publication. A levy on the developer may be considered as a means of covering part of the cost of this archaeological work.

3.8 In order to resolve historical problems by archaeological means, it is necessary to draw up a list of research priorities. Archaeologists need to be able to excavate not simply in advance of redevelopment, but also as part of a phased programme of scientific investigation.

3.9 With so many buildings either vacant or derelict a general move to acquire and redevelop the site of medieval Dublin on the same commercial lines as we see elsewhere in the modern city centre, controlled only by market forces and current planning procedures, would present an overwhelming threat to the archaeological wealth of Dublin. Quite simply, most of it would be destroyed without record.

3.10 The potential threat to the archaeological levels is immense, and full archaeological excavation in every case is not a practicable solution. It would cost more money and take more time than will ever be available. We must find another solution that permits redevelopment to go ahead but does not involve the destruction of archaeological levels. In other words, there should be an overall *planning* solution that will apply to the area as a whole leaving archaeological excavation as a selective tool to be employed in special cases only, either for purposes of research or where a particular development is of overriding importance.

3.11 In conjunction with an independent historical planning body, Dublin Corporation should assume responsibility for the welfare of the city's archaeological heritage, otherwise there is no prospect of an orderly development of the city's core area. If a planning solution to medieval Dublin's problems is to be enforced by the Corporation, it is first of all necessary that it be set out as an objective in the development plan.

3.12 The Dublin City Development Plan should contain a recognition of the existence and importance of the medieval town, with its inner core of pre-Norman settlement. This area should be treated as far as possible as a whole — at least as far as the underground remains are concerned. It should be thought of in certain respects as a conservation zone, and its needs should be promoted by the preparation of a special area plan, in which certain development guidelines would apply.

THE FUTURE CHARACTER OF MEDIEVAL DUBLIN

4.1 The Friends of Medieval Dublin are anxious that there should be suitable redevelopment in medieval Dublin in the near future. Because of their special interest in the area, they are particularly perturbed by the widespread dilapidation.

4.2 As befits a medieval town in a modern city, all existing medieval structures, as well as other old buildings of quality, should be incorporated in the new townscape.

4.3 The street pattern, which is of fundamental importance for the continuity of the area, should also be preserved. The objective should be to plan for the area as the historic core in its own right. Road widening to allow heavy traffic in transit is totally contradictory to those aims. Pedestrianisation has been used effectively in the medieval cores of other European cities. The alignment of the streets, as well as their width, should not be altered.

4.4 The scale and disposition of new buildings should enhance the existing buildings and should not conceal them, overshadow them, or detract from their essential economic and social functions.

4.5 A positive effort should be made to bring more life to the area by means of new mixed housing. The existing churches, schools and public houses, which are the principal old buildings on the site of medieval Dublin, should not be forced to close for lack of residents. These buildings are part, not merely of the traditional streetscape, but of the character of the area. Medieval Dublin must once again become a living city.

4.6 Future planning should allow for the uncovering and display *in situ* of important features of the medieval town, such as the sections of town wall and foundations of wall towers and gates that still lie underground.

RECOMMENDATIONS

In order to protect the heritage of medieval Dublin *and* to promote its modern development, we recommend:

1 That there be an active policy of appropriate redevelopment for the medieval city.

2 That in the next Dublin Draft Development Plan a new 'medieval core' area should be introduced corresponding to the full extent of the 'main zone of archaeological potential' shown on the Ordnance Survey map *Dublin c. 840-c. 1540*. This area includes 'sites of archaeological interest' listed in the plan and would reinforce their importance. This area should be given a quite specific protected status under planning law, within which special planning controls would apply, coupled with special incentives to encourage suitable kinds of building, which would exclude high-rise development destructive of the archaeological layers.

3 That as a matter of great urgency the road plans as indicated on the Dublin City Development Plan 1980 should be changed, because they are destructive of the historic core of the area, *both inside and outside the walls.*

4 That the Corporation should assume responsibility for the heritage of the city of Dublin and appoint an archaeological unit under a city and county archaeologist as exists, for instance, for cities such as Oxford and Southampton.

5 That the Corporation should commission a comprehensive sites and monuments record for the city and county of Dublin. The city archivist should be of considerable help in this project.

6 That the Corporation should promote a scheme for providing all sites of medieval

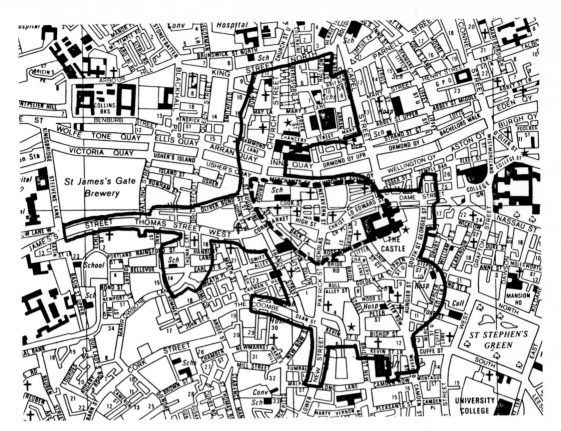

The extent of Dublin's medieval core. The area within the line should be treated as an archaeological zone and should be given protective status under planning law.

interest in the city and county with distinctive plaques, to inform Dubliners, enlighten visitors and encourage tourism in general.

7 That the Corporation should recognise the need for archaeological preservation and/or excavation by requiring the incorporation of appropriate clauses in contract documentation and planning permission.

8 That the Government should offer tax concessions to developers who would incorporate into their design plans the overall guidelines for the preservation of the special character of the medieval town.

9 That a major Museum of Dublin for the city and county be established, possibly based on a Civic Museum Trust, with a strong municipal representation on its council. In such a museum the results of the Dublin excavations would be communicated to the citizens of Dublin and to visitors.

Notes

CHAPTER 1

1 *Municipal Council of the City of Dublin: Reports* 1900, Vol. 3, pp 705-708; *Reports* 1901, Vol. 1, pp 287-9; *Minutes* 1901, p. 71 n. 97; ibid., p. 186 n. 233.

2 *Dublin of the Future: The New Town Plan,* Patrick Abercrombie, Sydney Kelly and Arthur Kelly, Vol. 1 of the *Publications of the Civics Institute of Ireland,* London, 1922, pp 37-38.

3 Ibid., p. xi and plate III.

4 *County Borough of Dublin and Neighbourhood Town Planning Report: Sketch Development Plan,* Patrick Abercrombie, Sydney A. Kelly and Manning Robertson, Dublin, 1941, p. 14.

5 Ibid., p. 38.

6 *The Lord Mayor's Handbook, Dublin Municipal Annual,* 1942, p. 27.

7 Report of an Coisde Cuspóirí Coiteann to Dublin City Council, No. 132, 1955, pp 519-20.

8 Report No. 109, 1951, adopted on 3 December 1951.

9 *Op. Cit.* in note 7, pp 521-2.

10 Ibid., p. 526.

11 Ibid., pp 527-8.

12 Report of An Coisde Cuspóirí Coiteann to Dublin City Council, No. 128, 1960, p. 480.

13 The Local Government (No. 2) Act, 1960.

14 Charles Haliday, *The Scandinavian Kingdom of Dublin,* Dublin, 2nd ed., 1884, pp 207-10.

15 (Marcus O hEochaide) Duplicated report on Archaeological Investigation at Dublin Castle, (7pp + Inventory of Finds (3p) + 7 figures + 25 plates), Office of Public Works, 1962. Various reports in the national press, Nov. 1961-Feb. 1962.

16 An attempt to show the extent of medieval Dublin has been made by The Friends of Medieval Dublin, and is published by the Ordnance Survey Office as *Dublin c. 840-c. 1540: The Medieval Town in the Modern City.*

17 *Irish Press, Irish Independent,* 19 November 1968.

18 Report of City Manager to Dublin City Council, No. 20, 1970, p. 100.

19 *Evening Press,* 7 November 1969.

20 *The Irish Times,* 30 January 1974.

21 Letter from Director of National Museum (A. T. Lucas) to Dublin Corporation (H. P. Byrne), 3 August 1972.

22 Report of City Manager to Dublin City Council, 6 December 1973, p. 4.

23 Report of City Manager to Dublin City Council, No. 76, 1973, p. 382.

24 Letter from Dublin Corporation (T. Ryan) to National Museum (A. T. Lucas), 16 May 1973.

25 (a) *Viking and Medieval Dublin, National Museum Excavations 1962-73,* Catalogue of Exhibition, 1973; (b) *Proceedings of the Seventh Viking Congress, Dublin 15-21 August, 1973,* ed., Bo Almqvist and David Greene, Dublin, 1976.

26 Letter from National Museum (A. T. Lucas) to National Monuments Advisory Council (F. Foley), 2 November 1973.

27 Minutes of meeting held 9 November 1973, *re* Wood Quay site, between representatives of National Museum and Corporation and their consultant architects.

28 *Op. Cit.* note 22, pp 5-6.

29 'Proposed Civic Office site to be kept as open space says Tully', *The Irish Times,* 22 January 1974.

30 'Corporation Offices allowed on first site', *The Irish Times,* 13 February 1974.

31 Minutes of meeting held 13 March 1974 *re* Civic Offices Site – Archaeological Implications, between National Museum, Corporation and consultant architects.

32 *The Irish Times/Irish Independent/Irish Press,* 14 March 1974.

33 'Destroying Dublin by Pussyfooting Tactics', Ian Blake, *The Irish Times,* 4 April 1974.

34 'On the adjournment', Senator Augustine Martin, 10 April 1974.

35 *The Irish Times,* 8 October 1974.

36 *The Irish Times,* 24 August 1974.

37 (a) 'Time is running out ...' (letter to the editor); (b) 'Digging for History' (leader); both in *The Irish Times,* 21 September 1974.

38 *The Irish Times,* 6 November 1974.

39 'Museum to preside over archaeological disaster', *Life and Environment,* No. 6, October 1974.

40 *The Irish Times,* 28 November 1974.

41 *Evening Press,* 11 January 1975.

42 Letter from National Museum (A. T. Lucas) to Dublin Corporation (P. Morrissey), 10 March 1975.

43 'Archaeologists granted six weeks more on Dublin site', *The Irish Times,* 2 April 1975.

44 'An Taisce head confronts Corporation PRO at site: alleges "institutionalised

vandalism'' of newly uncovered medieval ruins', *The Irish Times,* 8 April 1975.

45 'Old Dublin — Conservation and Preservation', 2 April 1975, (typescript statement by Dr Joseph Raftery, Keeper of Irish Antiquities at National Museum).

46 *Irish Press,* 9 April 1975.

47 *Irish Press,* 26 April 1975.

48 'A Report on Wood Quay for Professor R. D. Edwards', (unpublished typescript), 30 April 1975.

49 'Public dump is a source of rare museum pieces', *The Irish Times,* 3 May 1975.

50 *Irish Press,* 30 June 1975.

51 (a) 'Museum abandons the Wood Quay dig — 50 workers get the sack'; (b) 'Archaeological workers to be kept on', *The Irish Times,* 29 November 1975 and 3 December 1975.

52 Letter from Dublin Corporation (P. Russell) to National Museum (A. T. Lucas), 2 March 1976.

53 *The Irish Times,* 26 May 1976.

54 Letter from National Museum (A. T. Lucas) to Dublin Corporation (P. J. Russell), 7 July 1976.

55 'The Wood Quay Saga, part 1, November 1977-January 1979: Bulldozers and a National Monument', F. X. Martin, *The Belvederian,* 1979, pp 220-221.

CHAPTER 5

1 P. F. Wallace, 'The Archaeological Significance of Wood Quay, Dublin', *An Cosantóir* (The Irish Defence Journal), 1979, pp 141-7.

2 A. B. Ó Ríordáin, 'The High Street Excavations', in B. Almqvist and D. Greene (eds.), *Proceedings of the Seventh Viking Congress,* Dublin, 1976, pp 135-40; A. B. Ó Ríordáin, 'Aspects of Viking Dublin', in H. Bekker-Nielsen, P. Foote and O. Olsen (eds.), *Proceedings of the Eighth Viking Congress,* Odense, 1981, pp 43-4; H. Murray, 'Houses and Other Structures from the Dublin Excavations, 1962-76: A Summary', in H. Bekker-Nielsen et al. (eds.), *Proceedings Eighth Viking Congress,* Odense, 1981, pp 57-68; H. Murray, *Viking and Early Medieval Buildings in Dublin,* B.A.R. British Ser. 119, 1983.

3 P. F. Wallace, 'Carpentry in Ireland A.D. 900-1300 — The Wood Quay Evidence', in S. McGrail (ed.), *Woodworking Techniques before A.D. 1500,* B.A.R. Int. Ser. 129, 1982, pp 263-299 esp. pp 266-7; P. F. Wallace, 'Viking-age in Dublin', *British Heritage* 5, 1983-4, pp 37-41 and 54-5 esp. pp 40 and 54; P. F. Wallace, 'The Archaeology of Viking Dublin', in H. B. Clarke and A. Simms (eds.), *Comparative Urban Origins in Non-Roman Europe.* B.A.R. Int. Ser. Oxford 1985, pp 103-45; P. F. Wallace, 'Irish Early Christian "Wooden" Oratories — A

Suggestion', *N. Munster Antiq. Jr.,* 1982, pp 19-28.

4 P. F. Wallace, 'Carpentry in Ireland A.D. 900-1300 — The Wood Quay Evidence', pp 293-4.

5 P. F. Wallace, 'Dublin's Waterfront at Wood Quay: 900-1317', in G. Milne and B. Hobley (eds.), *Waterfront Archaeology in Britain and Northern Europe,* C.B.A. Research Report No. 41, 1981, pp 109-118.

6 P. F. Wallace, 'The Growth of 13th century Dublin', in *Dublin Arts Festival* 1974, pp 22-4.

7 C.f. footnote 4 *supra.*

8 M. Baillie, 'Dating of some ships' timbers from Wood Quay Dublin', in J. M. Fletcher (ed.), *Dendrochronology in Europe,* B.A.R. Int. Ser., 51, Oxford, 1978, pp 259-62.

9 P. F. Wallace, 'Iron tools and fittings in Viking-age Dublin', in B. G. Scott (ed.), *Proceedings of U.I.S.P.P. 1984 Symposium on 'The Craft of the Blacksmith'* forthcoming, Belfast.

10 E. Rynne, 'The Impact of the Vikings on Irish Weapons', *Atti del VI Congresso Internazionale delle Scienze Preistoriche e Protostoriche, Roma 1962,* Rome, 1966.

11 P. F. Wallace, 'A Catalogue of Dublin's Tenth to Thirteenth Century Weights with an account of their Production and Use', forthcoming.

12 P. F. Wallace, 'North European Pottery Imported into Dublin 1200-1500' in R. Hodges and P. J. Davey (eds.), *Ceramics and Trade, Sheffield 1983,* pp 225-230.

13 J. G. Hurst, 'Medieval Pottery Imported into Ireland'; K. J. Barton, 'Dublin's Medieval Pottery'; A. G. Vince, 'Early Medieval English Pottery in Dublin'; R. Ó Floinn, 'Handmade Medieval Pottery in S.E. Ireland — "Leinster Cooking Ware"', all in G. MacNiocaill and P. F. Wallace (eds.), *Keimelia: Studies in Archaeology and History in Memory of Tom Delaney,* Galway, forthcoming.

14 R. H. M. Dolley, *The Hiberno-Norse Coins in the British Museum,* London, 1966.

15 Cf. footnote 11 *supra.*

16 T. Fanning, 'Some aspects of the Bronze Ringed Pin in Scotland', in A. O'Connor and D. V. Clarke (eds.), *From the Stone Age to the 'Forty-Five,* Edinburgh, 1983, pp 324-42, esp. p. 331.

17 P. F. Wallace, 'The Origins of Dublin' in B. G. Scott (ed.), *Studies on Early Ireland,* Belfast, 1982, pp 129-43.

18 P. F. Wallace, 'The English presence in Viking Dublin' in M. Blackburn (ed.), *Michael Dolley Memorial Volume* forthcoming.

19 D. A. Binchy, 'The Passing of the Old Order', in B. Ó Cuiv (ed.), *Proceedings of the International Congress of Celtic Studies Dublin 1959,* Dublin, 1962, pp 119-132. A. T. Lucas, 'Irish-Norse Relations — Time for a

Reappraisal?', *Journal Cork Hist. Arch. Soc.*, 71, 1966, pp. 62-75.

20 P. F. Wallace, 'Anglo-Norman Dublin — Continuity and Change' in D. Ó Corráin (ed.), *Irish Antiquity*, Cork, 1982, pp 247-67.

21 J. F. Lydon, 'From Viking Settlement to Ostman town', unpublished presidential address to the Royal Society of Antiquaries of Ireland, 1982.

22 P. F. Wallace, 'The Archaeology of Viking Dublin', in H. B. Clarke and A. Simms (eds.), *Comparative History of Urban Origins in Non-Roman Europe*, B.A.R., Int. Ser., Oxford, 1985, pp 103-45.

23 P. F. Wallace, 'The Archaeology of Anglo-Norman Dublin', in H. B. Clarke and A. Simms (eds.), *The Comparative History of Urban Origins in Non-Roman Europe*, B.A.R. Int. Ser., Oxford, 1984, pp 379-410.

24 P. F. Wallace, 'Everyday Life in Viking Dublin', in *Limerick Association Yearbook*, 1984, pp 75-9.

CHAPTER 6

1 *Transactions of the Royal Irish Academy*, Vol. XXII, 1850, pp 437-451.

2 *History and Antiquities of the City of Dublin*, Dublin, 1766.

3 Holinshed, *Chronicles of England, Scotland, Wales and Ireland: the description of Ireland*, Lucas Harison, London 1577, p. 9.

CHAPTER 7

1 Georges Duby, *The Early Growth of the European Economy: Warriors and Peasants from the Seventh to the Twelfth Century*, trans H. B. Clarke, London, 1974, pp 112-39; A. T. Lucas, 'Irish-Norse relations: time for a reappraisal?', *Journal of the Cork Historical and Archaeological Society*, LXXI, 1966, pp 62-75, and the same author's 'The plundering and burning of churches in Ireland, seventh to sixteenth century' in Etienne Rynne (ed.), *North Munster Studies: Essays in Commemoration of Monsignor Michael Moloney*, Limerick, 1967, pp 172-229; Donncha Ó Corráin, *Ireland before the Normans*, The Gill History of Ireland, ed. James Lydon and Margaret MacCurtain, II, 1972, pp 82-9, 104-10; P. H. Sawyer, *The Age of the Vikings*, 2nd edn, London, 1971, pp 177-201.

2 G. A. Little, *Dublin before the Vikings: an Adventure in Discovery*, Dublin, 1957, pp 133-5, 147-8 and map facing p. 133. Even more bizarre is the concept of Dublin as a city of the 'Fluvial Epoch' outlined in Nuala Burke, *Dublin's Wood Quay*, Drumconrath, 1977, pp 11-26. No one should be misled by this aberrant and unsubstantiated mysticism.

3 H. B. Clarke, 'The topographical development of early medieval Dublin', *Journal of the Royal Society of Antiquaries of Ireland*, CVII, 1977, pp 29-51.

4 In response to letters written in May 1922, when the Four Courts and the Public Record Office were under military occupation, the council of the Royal Society of Antiquaries of Ireland received assurances from both sides 'that every precaution was being taken to insure that the documents, the importance of which was fully recognized, would not be interfered with' (*Journal of the Royal Society of Antiquaries of Ireland*, LIII [1923], p. 113).

5 H. B. Clarke, *Dublin c. 840 to c. 1540: the Medieval Town in the Modern City*, Dublin, 1978.

6 W. M. Hennessy and Bartholomew MacCarthy (eds.), *Annála Uladh: Annals of Ulster … a Chronicle of Irish Affairs from A.D. 431 to A.D. 1540*, Dublin, 1887-1901 (hereafter cited as *Annals of Ulster*), I, pp 344-5 (*sub anno* 840).

7 James Graham-Campbell, 'The Viking-age silver hoards of Ireland' in Bo Almqvist and David Greene (eds.), *Proceedings of the Seventh Viking Congress*, Dublin, 1976, p. 40.

8 The archaeological features shown on p. 149 are based on the plan printed in *The Irish Times*, 13 February and 8 March 1979. The precise location of many of the documented sites is uncertain.

9 *Annals of Ulster*, ed. Hennessy, I, pp 358-9 (*sub anno* 850), where the phrase *etir doine ocus moine* is used. The leader of this Danish expedition may have been the redoubtable Ragnarr Iodbrók (A. P. Smyth, *Scandinavian Kings in the British Isles, 850-880* Oxford, 1977, pp 90-2).

10 *Annals of Ulster*, ed. Hennessy, I, pp 416-7 (*sub annis* 901-2).

11 J. H. Todd (ed.), *Cogadh Gaedhel re Gallaibh: the War of the Gaedhil with the Gaill, or the Invasions of Ireland by the Danes and Other Norsemen: the Original Irish Text*, Rolls Series, XLVIII, 1867, pp 34-5.

12 *Annals of Ulster*, ed. Hennessy, I, pp 454-7 (*sub annis* 935-6); John O'Donovan (ed.), *Annála Ríoghachta Éireann: Annals of the Kingdom of Ireland, by the Four Masters, from the Earliest Period to the Year 1616*, Dublin, 1851 (hereafter cited as *Four Masters*), II, pp 630-3 (*sub anno* 934).

13 *Annals of Ulster*, ed. Hennessy, I, pp 456-9 (*sub annis* 937-8); *Four Masters*, ed. O'Donovan, II, pp 636-9 (*sub anno* 937). The precise sequence of events is unclear and the *Annals of Ulster* refer again to the plundering of Old Kilcullen *sub annis* 938-9.

14 *Annals of Ulster*, ed. Hennessy, I, pp 462-3 (*sub annis* 942-3); *Four Masters*, ed. O'Donovan, II, pp 646-9 (*sub anno* 941). The verse passage in the *Annals of the Four Masters* says that Lorcán was killed in a wretched house (*i ttreibh troch*).

15 *Annals of Ulster*, ed. Hennessy, I, pp 462-5 (*sub annis* 943-4); *Four Masters*, ed.

O'Donovan, II, pp 650-3 (*sub anno* 942).

16 *Annals of Ulster,* ed. Hennessy, I, pp 472-3 (*sub annis* 955-6); *Four Masters,* ed. O'Donovan, II, pp 656-9 (*sub anno* 945), 672-5 (*sub anno* 954).

17 *Four Masters,* ed. O'Donovan, II, pp 710-13 (*sub anno* 979), 732-5 (*sub anno* 994).

18 *Annals of Ulster,* ed. Hennessy, I, pp 504-5 (*sub annis* 997-8); *Four Masters,* ed. O'Donovan, II, pp 736-7 (*sub anno* 997).

19 *Annals of Ulster,* ed. Hennessy, I, pp 506-7 (*sub annis* 998-9); *Four Masters,* ed. O'Donovan, II, pp 738-41 (*sub anno* 998). The *Annals of Ulster* attribute these exploits to Brian and his forces, but there is support for the *Annals of the Four Masters* in W. M. Hennessy (ed.), *Chronicon Scotorum: a Chronicle of Irish Affairs from the Earliest Times to A.D. 1135, with a Supplement containing the Events from 1141 to 1150,* Rolls Series, XLVI, 1866 (hereafter cited as *Chronicon Scotorum*), pp 236-7.

20 *Four Masters,* ed. O'Donovan, II, pp 782-3 (*sub anno* 1014).

21 On Dublin's role in the slave trade see Smyth, *Scandinavian Kings in the British Isles,* pp 154-6, 158-9, 166-8.

22 *Chronicon Scotorum,* ed. Hennessy, pp 232-3; *Four Masters,* ed. O'Donovan, II, pp 722-5.

23 *Four Masters,* ed. O'Donovan, II, pp 782-3 (*sub anno* 1014): '... co ro loisccseat an dún, ocus gach araibhe ó dún amach do thaighibh'.

24 J. K. Clarke, 'The parish of St Olave', *Dublin Historical Record,* XI, 1949-50, pp 118-9. The author commented: 'the authorities of the National Museum were notified, but the result[s] of their investigations, if any, do not appear to have been published' (ibid).

25 Ibid., p. 121. The chamber and church occupied respectively the sites of what later became 40 and 41 Fishamble Street. *Cf.* Richard Haworth's letter to *The Irish Times,* 10 October 1977.

26 *Four Masters,* ed. O'Donovan, II, pp 1176-7: '... a nár ar lár a ndúine féin'.

27 P. F. Wallace, 'Wood Quay: the growth of thirteenth-century Dublin' in *Dublin Arts Festival 1976,* Dublin, 1976, pp 22-4; P. F. Wallace, 'Dublin's waterfront at Wood Quay 900-1317' in G. Milne and B. Hobley (eds.), *Waterfront Archaeology in Britain and Northern Europe,* London, 1981, pp 109-18. The quay-wall should be distinguished from any defensive structures built later along the hitherto open quay. The river frontage between Bridge Gate and Fyan's Castle may have been provided with stone defences at the time of the Bruce emergency in 1317. Speed's bird's-eye-view plan shows a wall with gaps that presumably gave access to the riverside (John Speed, *The Theatre of the Empire of Great Britaine . . .* London, 1611, following p. 141).

28 Nuala Burke, 'Dublin's north-eastern city wall: early reclamation and development at the Poddle-Liffey confluence', *Proceedings of the Royal Irish Academy,* LXXIV, 1974, section C, pp 113-32 is an important contribution based on documentary analysis and was published after the National Museum had abandoned the site in July 1973.

29 J. T. and R. M. Gilbert (eds.), *Calendar of Ancient Records of Dublin in Possession of the Municipal Corporation of that City,* Dublin and London, 1889-1944, I, pp 106, 109-10.

30 Ibid., pp 5, 104, 164.

31 Ibid., p. 223; J. T. Gilbert (ed.), *Historic and Municipal Documents of Ireland, A.D. 1172-1320,* Rolls Series, LIII, 1870, p. 239: '... una venella iacet ab ecclesia sancti Johannis a Bouestrete usque ad portam in vico taberne'.

32 John Rocque, *An Exact Survey of the City and Suburbs of Dublin ...,* Dublin, 1756. This map has been republished with an introduction by J. H. Andrews under the title *Two Maps of Eighteenth-century Dublin and its Surroundings,* Lympne, 1977.

33 Public Record Office, *The Twenty-third Report of the Deputy Keeper of the Public Records in Ireland* (Dublin, 1891), p. 150. Only 24 per cent of the Anglo-Norman deposits between the Hiberno-Norse wall and the Liffey were fully excavated. The enormous scale of the destruction of archaeological material on the Wood Quay site is detailed in N. C. Maxwell's letter to *The Irish Times,* 31 March 1979.

34 Gilbert, *Calendar of Ancient Records of Dublin,* I, p. 290.

35 Ibid., II, pp 555-6.

36 William Reeves, *Memoir of the Church of St Duilech . . .,* Dublin, 1859, p. 5.

37 J. H. Todd, introduction to J. C. Crosthwaite (ed.), *The Book of Obits and Martyrology of the Cathedral Church of the Holy Trinity . . .,* Dublin, 1844, pp lxxx-lxxxiii. I am grateful to Richard Haworth for drawing my attention to this discussion.

38 P. H. Hore, *History of the Town and County of Wexford,* V, London, 1906, pp 76, 178, 181 (St Tullock's).

CHAPTER 8
Select Bibliography

J. Andrews, 'The Oldest Map Of Dublin', *Proceedings of The Royal Irish Academy,* Sect. C, Vol. 83, 1983, pp 205-237.

M. W. Barley, *European Towns: Their Archaeology and History,* Academic Press, London 1977.

T. Barry, 'Wood Quay, Dublin', *Current Archaeology* 66, London 1979, pp 209-211.

H. B. Clarke, 'The topographical development of early medieval Dublin', *Journal of the Royal Society of Antiquaries of Ireland,* 107, 1977, pp 29-51.

H. B. Clarke, *Dublin c.840 to c.1540, The Medieval Town in the Modern City,* Ordnance Survey, Dublin, 1978

H. B. Clarke and A. Simms, 'Early Dublin 790 to 1170' and 'Medieval Dublin', T. W. Moody, F. X. Martin and F. Byrne: *A New History of Ireland,* IX, Oxford, 1984, pp 36 and 37.

H. B. Clarke and A. Simms (eds.), *The Comparative History of Urban Origins in Non-Roman Europe: Ireland, Wales, Denmark, Germany, Poland and Russia from the Ninth to the Thirteenth Century,* British Archaeol. Reports, Oxford, 2 vols., 1985.

Corporation of Dublin, *Dublin City Development Plan,* Draft Review 1980.

Curriculum Development Unit, T.C.D., *Viking Settlement to Medieval Dublin. Daily life 840-1540,* Dublin, 1978.

L. De Paor, 'Viking Dublin', in *Dublin Historical Record,* 1978, pp 142-145.

E. Gibson, 'Understanding the Subjective Meaning of Places', in *Humanistic Geography,* ed. D. Ley and M. S. Samuels, London, 1978.

J. T. Gilbert and R. M. Gilbert, *Calendar of ancient records of Dublin in possession of the municipal corporation of that city,* Dublin and London, 1889-1922, 19 vols.

P. Healy, The town walls of Dublin, in E. Gillespie (ed.), *The Liberties of Dublin,* Dublin, 1973, pp 16-23.

W. Hensel, 'The origin of Western and Eastern Slav towns', *World Archaeology,* 1, 1969-70, pp 51-60.

W. Hensel, The Origins of Western and Eastern European Slav Towns, in M. W. Barley (ed.): *European Towns, Their Archaeology and Early History,* Academic Press, 1977, pp 373-390.

J. Herrmann, 'Research into Early History of the town in the Territory of the German Democratic Republic', in *European Towns,* ed. by M. W. Barley, 1977.

H. Jankuhn, 'Trade and settlement in Central and Northern Europe up to and during the Viking period', *Journal of the Royal Society of Antiquaries of Ireland,* 112, 1982, pp 18-50.

H. Jankuhn, W. Schlesinger and H. Steuer (eds.), *Vor - und Frühformen der Europaischen Stadt in Mittelalter,* Akademie der Wissenschaften Göttingen, Vol. I, 1975, Vol. II, 1974.

H. Jankuhn, *Haithabu,* Neumünster, 1972.

N. Maxwell (ed.), *Digging up Dublin,* Dublin, 1980.

C. McNeill (ed.), *Calendar of Archbishop Alen's Register, c.1172-1534,* Royal Society of Antiquaries, extra volume, 1950.

B. Meehan, R. Walsh and J. Molloy, 'Urban Regeneration and Dublin's Medieval City: The Urban Development Area Bill: Is it the Way Forward?, in J. Blackwell and F. J. Convery (eds.), *Promise and Performance,* Dublin, 1983, pp. 313-334.

H. Murray, *Viking and Early Medieval Buildings in Dublin,* British Archaeological Reports, British Series, 119, 1983.

R. N. Newcomb, *Planning the Past: Studies in Historical Geography,* editors A. H. Baker and F. B. Harley, Dawson 1979.

B. Ó Ríordáin, 'The High Street Excavations', in: B. Almqvist and D. Green (eds.): *Proceedings of the Seventh Viking Congress,* Dublin, 1976, pp 135-140.

A. Percival, *Understanding our Surroundings: A manual of urban interpretation,* London, 1979.

E. Relph, *Place and placelessness,* London, 1976.

A. Simms, 'Medieval Dublin: A Topographical Analysis', in *Irish Geography,* Vol. 12, 1979, pp 25-41.

A. Simms, 'Defining the significance of the Inner City', in J. Blackwell and F. J. Convery (eds.), *Promises and Performance,* Dublin, 1983, pp 303-312.

A. P. Smyth, *Scandinavian York and Dublin: The History and Archaeology of two related Viking Kingdoms,* Vol. 1, Dublin 1975, Vol 2, 1979.

J. Speed, *The Theatre of the Empire of Great Britaine . . .,* London, 1611.

F. Tilden, *Interpreting our heritage,* Chapel Hill, New York, 1967.

P. F. Wallace, 'Anglo-Norman Dublin: Continuity and Change', in D. O Corráin, ed., *Irish Antiquity,* Cork, 1981, pp 247-267.

P. F. Wallace, 'The Origins of Dublin', in B. G. Scott (ed.) *Studies on Early Ireland: Essays in Honour of M. V. Duignan,* 1982, pp 129-143.

P. F. Wallace, 'The Archaeology of Viking Dublin' and 'The Archaeology of Anglo-Norman Dublin', in H. B. Clarke and A. Simms (eds.), *The Comparative History of Urban Origins in Non-Roman Europe, Ireland, Wales, Denmark, Germany, Poland and Russia from the Ninth to the Thirteenth Century,* British Archaeological Reports, Oxford 1985, pp 103-45, 379-410.

P. Walsh, *Dublin c.840 to 1540: the years of medieval growth,* Ordnance Survey, Dublin, 1977.

M. Wright, *The Dublin Region,* Advisory Regional Plan and Final Report, Dublin, 1967.

Our heritage is an investment. If safeguarded now it will be enjoyed for years to come.

PICTURE CREDITS

We would like to thank those who gave permission to reproduce illustrations. These are listed below, together with the other sources of illustration, where traceable. Some illustrations are acknowledged with the text.

Abercrombie New Town Plan, 1922 17; Abercrombie Sketch Development Plan, 1941 19 top + bot. left; *Architectural Review: A Future for Dublin,* 1974 19 bot. right, 23; Pat Brereton 155; Eddie Buckmaster 63 bot.; *Calendar of Ancient Records of Dublin* 13, 145; H. B. Clarke 149; John De Courcy 165; Brian Doyle 43 top left; *Dublin Penny Journal,* 1832 169, 1834 170; *Evening Press* 25; Bob Fannin 26, 52, 184; Brooke Givot 35 bot.; George Gmelch 173 top; *Hall's Ireland* 12, 171; *Irish Independent* 84, 184; *The Irish Press* 10/11, 29, 53, 70, 72, 73; *The Irish Times* 1, 2, 14, 33, 37, 39, 43 top, 44/45, 46, 59 top, 63 top, 69, 74, 75, 77, 79, 86, 88 top, 91 top right, 173 bot., 174, 183; G. Little, *Dublin Before the Vikings* 146; Jean Mattson 59 bot., 66, 70 top, 91 top left; National Museum of Ireland 7, 113 bot., 114, 115, 117, 135, 136, 138, 141, 142, 143; (V. Dowling) 118 bot., 131, 132; (B. P. Doyle) 122 bot., 127; (P. F. Wallace) 113 top, 118 top, 122 top; Michael O'Brien 35 top; Ordnance Survey of Ireland 177; Claire O'Reilly 82, 87, 89; Tom O'Riordáin 90; Nick Robinson 67; Anngret Simms 156, 159 (top), 161, 162; G.E. Street, *Christ Church Cathedral* (1882) 150; *The Sunday Press* 84; *Sunday World* 57 bot.; Leo Swan 160; Martyn Turner + *The Irish Times* 49. Photographs used on front and back covers are used with permission of *The Irish Times.*

'And on your right is Wood Quay — scene of the last Viking battle back in the 1980s.'

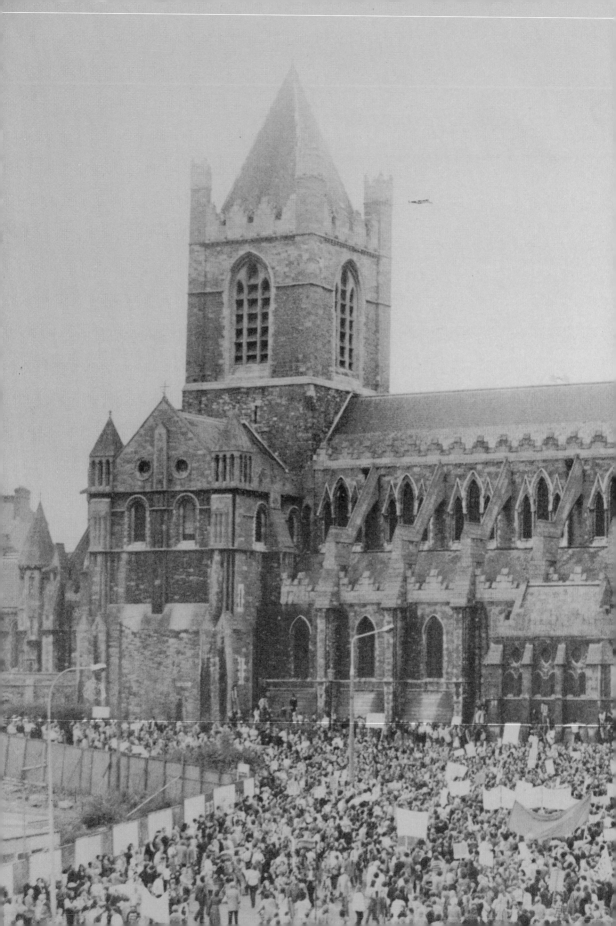